PART ONE

A SCHOOL HISTORY

OF THE

Negro Race in America

FROM 1619 TO 1890

COMBINED WITH THE HISTORY OF THE
NEGRO SOLDIERS IN THE SPANISH-AMERICAN
WAR, ALSO A SHORT SKETCH OF LIBERIA

BY

EDWARD A. JOHNSON

REVISED EDITION, 1911

AMS PRESS
NEW YORK

Reprinted from a copy in the New York Public Library
Schomburg Collection
From the edition of 1911, Raleigh
First AMS EDITION published 1969
Manufactured in the United States of America

Library of Congress Catalogue Card Number: 73-100532

AMS PRESS, INC.
New York, N.Y. 10003

PREFACE.

To the many thousand colored teachers in our country this book is dedicated. During my experience of eleven years as a teacher, I have often felt that the children of the race ought to study some work that would give them a little information on the many brave deeds and noble characters of their own race. I have often observed the sin of omission and commission on the part of white authors, most of whom seem to have written exclusively for white children, and studiously left out the many creditable deeds of the Negro. The general tone of most of the histories taught in our schools has been that of the inferiority of the Negro, whether actually said in so many words, or left to be implied from the highest laudation of the deeds of one race to the complete exclusion of those of the other. It must, indeed, be a stimulus to any people to be able to refer to their ancestors as distinguished in deeds of valor, and peculiarly so to the colored people. But how must the little colored child feel when he has completed the assigned course of U. S. History and in it found not one word of credit, not one word of

favorable comment for even one among the millions
of his foreparents, who have lived through nearly
three centuries of his country's history! The Negro
is hardly given a passing notice in many of the histories taught in the schools; he is credited with no
heritage of valor; he is mentioned only as a slave,
while true historical records prove him to have been
among the most patriotic of patriots, among the
bravest of soldiers, and constantly a God-fearing,
faithful producer of the nation's wealth. Though
a slave to this government, his was the first blood
shed in its defence in those days when a foreign foe
threatened its destruction. In each of the American
wars the Negro was faithful—yes, faithful to a land
not his own in point of rights and freedom, but, indeed, a land that, after he had shouldered his musket to defend, rewarded him with a renewed term
of slavery. Patriotism and valor under such circumstances possess a peculiar merit and beauty. But
such is the truth of history; and may I not hope that
the study of this little work by the boys and girls of
the race will inspire in them a new self-respect and
confidence? Much, of course, will depend on you,
dear teachers, into whose hands I hope to place this
book. By your efforts, and those of the children,
you are to teach from the truth of history that com-
plexions do not govern patriotism, valor, and sterling
integrity.

My endeavor has been to shorten this work as much as I thought consistent with clearness. Personal opinions and comments have been kept out. A fair impartial statement has been my aim. Facts are what I have tried to give without, bias or prejudice; and may not something herein said hasten on that day when the race for which these facts are written, following the example of the noble men and women who have gone before, level themselves up to the highest pinnacle of all that is noble in human nature?

I respectfully request that my fellow-teachers will see to it that the word *Negro* is written with a capital *N*. It deserves to be so enlarged, and will help, perhaps, to magnify the race it stands for in the minds of those who see it.

E. A. J.

CONTENTS—PART I.

A SCHOOL HISTORY

OF THE

NEGRO RACE IN AMERICA.

CHAPTER I.

INTRODUCTION.

The Origin of the Negro is definitely known. Some very wise men, writing to suit prejudiced readers, have endeavored to assign the race to a separate creation and deny its kindred with Adam and Eve. But historical records prove the Negro as ancient as the most ancient races—for 5000 years into the dim past mention is made of the Negro race. *The pyramids of Egypt*, the great temples on the Nile, were either built by Negroes or people closely related to them. *All the science and learning* of ancient Greece and Rome was, probably, once in the hands of the foreparents of the American slaves. They are, then, descendants of a race of people once the most powerful on earth, the race of the Pharaohs. History, traced from the flood, makes the three sons of Noah, Ham, Shem, and Japheth, the progenitors of the three primitive races of the earth—the Mongolian, descended from Shem and settled in Southern and Eastern Asia; the Caucasian, descended from Japheth and settled in Europe; the Ethiopian, descended from Ham and settled in Africa and adjacent countries. *From Ham undoubtedly* sprung the Egyptians who, in honor of Ham, their great head, named their principal god *Hammon or Ammon*.

Ham was the father of Canaan, from whom descended the powerful Canaanites so troublesome to the Jews. *Cush*, the oldest son of Ham, was the father of Nimrod, "the mighty one in the earth" and founder of the Babylonian Empire. Nimrod's son built the unrivalled City of Nineveh in the picturesque valley of the Tigris. Unless the Bible statement be false that "*God created of one blood all nations of men for to dwell on the face of the earth,*" and the best historians have erred, then the origin of the Negro is high enough to merit his proudest boasts of the past, and arouse his grandest hopes for the future.

The Present Condition of the African is the result of the fall of the Egyptian empire, which was in accord with the Bible prophecy of all nations who forgot God and worshipped idols. That the Africans were once a great people is shown by their natural love for the fine arts. They are poetic by nature, and national airs sung long ago by exploring **parties in Central Africa are** still held by them, and strike the ears of more modern travellers with joy and surprise.

Ancient Cities Discovered in the very heart of Africa, having well laid off streets, improved wharfs, and conveniences for trade, connect these people with a better condition in the past than now. While many of the native Africans are desperately savage, yet in their poor, degraded condition it is the unanimous testimony of missionaries and explorers that many of these people have good judgment, some tribes have written languages, and show skill in weaving cloth, smelting and refining gold and iron and making implements of war.

Their Wonderful regard for *truth and virtue* is surprising, and fixes a great gulf between them and other savage peoples. They learn rapidly, and, unfortunately, it is too often the case that evil teaching is given them by the vile traders who frequent their country with an abundance of rum, mouths full of curses, and the worst of bad English.

Long Years Spent in the most debilitating climate on earth and violation of divine law, made the African what he was when the slave trade commenced in the 16th century. But his condition was not so bad that he could not be made a good citizen. Nay, he was superior to the ancient savage Briton whom Cæsar found in England and described as unfitted to make respectable slaves of in the Roman

Empire.   The Briton has had eighteen centuries to be what he is, the Negro has had really but twenty-five years.   Let us weigh his progress in just balances.

SOME QUOTATIONS FROM LEADING WRITERS ON THE NEGRO.

"The Sphinx may have been the shrine of the Negro population of Egypt, who, as a people, were unquestionably under our average size.   Three million Buddhists in Asia represent their chief deity. Buddha, with Negro features and hair.   There are two other images of Buddha, one at Ceylon and the other at Calanse, of which Lieutenant Mahoney says: 'Both these statues agree in having crisped hair and long, pendant ear-rings.'"—*Morton.*

"The African is a man with every attribute of humankind.   Centuries of barbarism have had the same hurtful effects on Africans as Pritchard describes them to have had on certain of the Irish who were driven, some generations back, to the hills in Ulster and Connaught"—*the moral and physical effects are the same.*

"Ethnologists reckon the African as by no means the lowest of the human family.   He is nearly as strong physically as the European; and, as a race, is wonderfully persistent among the nations of the earth. Neither the diseases nor the ardent spirits which proved so fatal to the North American Indians, the South Sea Islanders and Australians, seem capable of annihilating the Negroes. They are gifted with physical strength capable of withstanding the severest privations. Many would pine away in a state of slavery. No Krooman can be converted into a slave, and yet he is an inhabitant of the low, unhealthy west coast; nor can any of the Zulu or Kaffir tribe be reduced to bondage, though all these live in comparatively elevated regions. We have heard it stated by men familiar with some of the Kaffirs, that a blow given, even in play, by a European, must be returned. A love of liberty is observable in all who have the Zulu blood, as the Makololo, the Watuta. But blood does not explain the fact. A beautiful Barotse woman at Naliele, on refusing to marry a man whom she did not like, was, in a pet, given by the headman to some Mambari slave traders from Benguela. Seeing her fate, she seized one of their spears, and, stabbing herself, fell dead."—*Livingstone's Works.*

"In ancient times the blacks were known to be so gentle to strangers that many believed that the gods sprang from them. Homer sings of the ocean, father of the gods, and says that when Jupiter wishes to take a holiday, he visits the sea, and goes to the banquets of the blacks—a people humble, courteous and devout."

THE CURSE OF NOAH WAS NOT DIVINE!

The following passage of Scripture has been much quoted as an argument to prove the inferiority of the Negro race. The Devil can quote Scripture, but not always correctly: "And Noah began to be an husbandman, and he planted a vineyard: and he drank of the wine, and was drunken and was uncovered in his tent, and Ham, the father of Canaan, saw the nakedness of his father, and told his two brethren without, and Shem and Japheth took a garment and laid it upon both their shoulders, and went backward and covered the nakedness of their father; and their faces were backward, and they saw not their father's nakedness, and Noah awoke from his wine, and knew what his younger son had done unto him, and he said, Cursed be Canaan; a servant of servants shall he be unto his brethren. And he said: Blessed be the Lord God of Shem, and Canaan shall be his servant. God shall enlarge Japheth, and he shall dwell in the tents of Shem, and Canaan shall be his servant."

After the flood Noah's mission as a preacher to the people was over. He so recognized it himself, and settled himself down with his family on a vineyard. He got drunk of the wine he made, and disgracefully lay in nakedness; on awaking from his drunken stupor, and learning of Ham's acts, he, in rage, speaks his feelings to Canaan, Ham's son. He was in bad temper at this time, and spoke as one in such a temper in those times naturally would speak. To say he was uttering God's will would be a monstrosity—would be to drag the sacred words of prophecy through profane lips, and make God speak his will to men out of the mouth of a drunkard, of whom the Holy Writ says none can enter the kingdom. A drunken prophet strikes the mind with ridicule! Yet, such was Noah, if at all, and such the character of that prophet whom biased minds have chosen as the expounder of a curse on the Negro race. It is not strange that so few people have championed the curse theory of the race, when we think that in so doing they must at the same time endorse Noah's drunkenness.

But, aside from this, the so-called prophecy of Noah has not become true The best evidence of a prophecy is its fulfillment. Canaan's descendants have often conquered, though Noah said they would not. Goodrich makes the Canaanites, so powerful in the fortified cities of Ai and Jericho, the direct descendants of Canaan They were among the most powerful people of olden times. They and their kindred built up Egypt, Phœnicia, the mother of the alphabet, and Nineveh and Babylon, the two most wonderful of ancient cities. The Jews, God's chosen people, were enslaved by the kindred of Canaan both in Egypt and Babylon. Melchizedek (King of Righteousness), a sacred character of the Old Testament, was a Canaanite. So, rather than being a race of slaves, as Noah predicted, the Canaanitish people have been the greatest people of the earth. The great nations of antiquity were in and around Eastern Africa and Western Asia, in which is located Mount Ararat, supposed to be the spot on which the ark rested after the flood. These nations sprang from the four sons of Ham—Cush, Mizarim, Phut and Canaan. The Cushites were Ethiopians, who lived in Abyssinia. The Mizarimites were Egyptians, who lived in Egypt, and so distinguished for greatness. The Canaanites occupied the country including Tyre and Sidon and stretching down into Arabia as far as Gaza and including the province of the renowned Queen of Sheba.

In the light of true history the curse theory of the Negro melts like snow under a summer's sun. We contend, from the above facts, that Noah did not utter a prophecy when he spoke to Canaan, and as proof of that fact we have quoted some historical data to show that if he did make such a prophecy it was not fulfilled. We will add, further, that the part of the alleged prophecy conferring blessings on Shem and Japheth has also fallen without verification, in that the descendants of these two personages have more than once been enslaved.

It seems hardly necessary in this age of enlightenment to refer to the *Curse Theory* argued so persistently by those who needed some such argument as an apology for wrong-doing, but still there are some who yet believe in it, having never cut loose from the moorings of blind prejudice. *The Color Theory* was also quite popular formerly as an argument in support of the curse of Noah. We hold that the color of the race is due to climatic influences, and in support of this view read this quotation in reference to Africa : " As we go westward we observe the light color predominating over the dark ; and then, again, when we come within the influence of the damp from the sea air, we find the shade deepened into the general blackness of the coast population.

" It is well known that the Biseagan women are shining white, the inhabitants of Granada, on the contrary, dark, to such an extent that in this region (West Europe) the pictures of the Blessed Virgin and other saints are painted of the same color."

Black is no mark of reproach to people who do not worship white. The West Indians in the interior represent the devil as *white.* The American Indians make fun of the "pale face," and so does the native African. People in this country have been educated to believe in white because all that is good has been ascribed to the white race both in pictures and words. God, the angels and all the prophets are pictured white and the Devil is represented as black.

CHAPTER II.

THE BEGINNING OF SLAVERY IN THE COLONIES.

The first Negroes landed at Jamestown, Va. In the year 1619, a Dutch trading vessel, being in need of supplies, weighed anchor at Jamestown, and exchanged fourteen Negroes for food and supplies. The Jamestown people made slaves of these *fourteen Negroes*, but did not pass any law to that effect until the year 1662, when the number of slaves in the colony was then nearly 2000, most of whom had been imported from Africa.

How They were Employed. The Jamestown colony early discovered the profits of the tobacco crop, and the Negro slaves were largely employed in this industry, where they proved very profitable. They were also enlisted in the militia, but could not bear arms except in defence of the colonists against the Indians. The greater part of the manual labor of all kinds was performed by the slaves.

The Slaves Imported came chiefly from the west coast of Africa. They were crowded into the holds of ships in droves, and often suffered for food and drink.   Many, when opportunity permitted, would jump overboard rather than be taken from their homes.   Various schemes were resorted to by the slave-traders to get possession of the Africans. They bought many who had been taken prisoners by stronger tribes than their own; they stole others, and some they took at the gun and pistol's mouth.

Many of the Captives of the slave-traders sold in this country were from tribes possessing more or less knowledge of the use of tools.   Some came from tribes skilled in making gold and ivory ornaments, cloth, and magnificent steel weapons of war. The men had been trained to truthfulness, honesty, and valor, while the women were virtuous even unto death.   While polygamy is prevalent among most African tribes, yet their system of marrying off the young girls at an early age, and thus putting them under the guardianship of their husbands, is a protection to them; and the result is plainly seen by travellers who testify positively to the uprightness of the women.

The Ancestors of the American Negroes, though savage in some respects, yet were not so bad as many people think.   The native African had then, and he has now, much respect for what we call **law and justice.**   This fact is substantiated by the numerous large tribes existing, individuals of which grow to be very old, a thing that could not happen were there the wholesale brutalism which we are sometimes told exists. All native Africans universally despise slavery, and even in Liberia have a contempt for the colored people there who were once slaves in America.

The Jamestown Slaves were doomed to servitude and ignorance both by law and custom; they were not allowed to vote, and could not be set free even by their masters, except for "some meritorious service." Their religious instruction was of an inferior order, and slaves were sometimes given to the white ministers as pay for their services.

The Free Negroes of Jamestown were in a similar condition to that of the slaves. They could vote and bear arms in defence of the colony, but not for themselves. They were taxed to bear the expenses of the government, but could not be educated in the schools they helped to build. Some of them managed to acquire some education and property.

The Negro Heroes who may have exhibited their heroism in many a daring feat during the early history of Jamestown are not known. It is unfortunate that there was no record kept except that of the crimes of his ancestors in this country. Judging, however, from the records of later years, we may conclude that the Negro slave of Jamestown was not without his Banneka or Blind Tom. Certainly his labor was profitable and may be said to have built up the colony.

When John Smith became Governor of the Jamestown colony, there were none but white inhabitants; their indolent habits caused him to make a law declaring that "he who would not work should not eat." Prior to this time the colony had proved a failure and continued so till the introduction of the slaves, under whose labor it soon grew prosperous and recovered from its hardships.

Thomas Fuller, sometimes called "the Virginia Calculator," must not be overlooked in speaking of the record of the Virginia Negro. He was stolen from his home in Africa and sold to a planter near Alexandria, Va. His genius for mathematics won for him a great reputation. He attracted the attention of such men as Dr. Benjamin Rush, of Philadelphia, who, in company with others, was passing through Virginia. Tom was sent for by one of the company and asked, "how many seconds a man of seventy years, some odd months, weeks and days, had lived?" He gave the exact number in a minute and a half. The gentleman who questioned him took his pen, and after some figuring told him he must be mistaken, as the number was too great. "'Top, massa!" cried Tom, "you hab left out the

leap year"—and sure enough Tom was correct.—
Williams.

The following was published in several newspapers when Thomas Fuller died:

" DIED.—Negro Tom, the famous African Calculator, aged 80 years. He was the property of Mrs.
Elizabeth Cox, of Alexandria. Tom was a very
black man. He was brought to this country at the
age of fourteen, and was sold as a slave with many
of his unfortunate countrymen. This man was a
prodigy; though he could neither read nor write, he
had perfectly acquired the use of enumeration. He
could give the number of months, days, weeks, hours,
minutes, and seconds for any period of time that a
person chose to mention allowing in his calculations
for all the leap years that happened in the time. He
would give the number of poles, yards, feet, inches
and barleycorns in a given distance—say the diam-
eter of the earth's orbit—and in every calculation he
would produce the true answer in less time than
ninety-nine out of a hundred men would take with
their pens. And what was, perhaps, more extraordinary, though interrupted in the progress of his calculations and engaged in discourse upon any other
subject, his operations were not thereby in the least
deranged. He would go on where he left off, and
could give any and all of the stages through which
his calculations had passed. Thus died Negro Tom,

this untaught arithmetician, this untutored scholar. Had his opportunities of improvement been equal to those of a thousand of his fellow-men, neither the Royal Society of London, the Academy of Sciences at Paris, nor even a Newton himself need have been ashamed to acknowledge him a brother in science."

How many of his kind might there have been had the people of Jamestown seen fit to give the Negroes who came to their shores a laborer's and emigrant's chance rather than enslaving them! Much bloodshed and dissension might thus have been avoided, and the honor of the nation never besmirched with human bondage.

CHAPTER III.

THE NEW YORK COLONY.

THE enslavement of the Negro seems to have commenced in the New York Colony about the same time as at Jamestown (1619). The slaves were used on the farms, and became so profitable that about the time the English took the colony from the Dutch, 1664, there was a great demand for slaves, and the trade grew accordingly.

The Privileges of the Slaves in New York were, for a while, a little better than in Virginia. They were taken into the church and baptized, and no law was passed to prevent their getting an education. But the famous Wall Street, now the financial centre of the New World, was once the scene of an auction block where Indians and persons of Negro descent were bought and sold. A whipping boss was once a characteristic officer in New York city.

The Riot of 1712 shows the feeling between the master and servant at that time. The Negro population being excluded from schools, not allowed to own land, even when free, and forbidden to "strike a Christian or Jew" in self-defence, and their testimony excluded from the courts, arose in arms and with the torch; houses were burned, and many whites killed, before the militia suppressed them. Many of the Negroes of New York were free, and many came from the Spanish provinces.

CHAPTER IV.

MASSACHUSETTS, RHODE ISLAND, AND CONNECTICUT.

NEGRO slavery existed in Massachusetts as early as 1633. The Puritan fathers who came to this country in search of liberty, carried on for more than a century a traffic in human flesh and blood. The New England ships of the 17th century brought cargoes of Negroes from the west coast of Africa and the Barbadoès. They sold many of them in New England as well as in the Southern colonies. In 1764 there were nearly 6000 slaves in Massachusetts, about 4000 in Rhode Island, and the same in Connecticut.

The Treatment of the slaves in these colonies at this time was regulated by laws which classed them as property, " being rated as horses and hogs." They could not bear arms nor be admitted to the schools. They were baptized in the churches, but this did not make them freemen, as it did white serfs.

Better Treatment was given the slaves as the colonies grew older and were threatened with wars

It was thought that the slaves might espouse the cause of the enemy, and for this reason some leniency was shown them, and the conscience of the people was also being aroused.

Judge Samuel Sewall, a Chief Justice of Massachusetts wrote a tract in 1700 warning the people of New England against slavery and ill treatment of Negroes. He said: "Forasmuch as Liberty is in real value next unto Life, none ought to part with it themselves, or deprive others of it, but upon most mature consideration."

Judge Sewall's tract greatly excited the New England people on the subject of emancipating their slaves. "The pulpit and the press were not silent, and sermons and essays in behalf of the enslaved Africans were continually making their appearance."

The Slaves Themselves aroused by these favorable utterances from friendly people made up petitions which they presented with strong arguments for their emancipation. A great many slaves brought suits against their masters for restraining them of their liberty. In 1774 a slave "of one Caleb Dodge," of Essex county, brought suit against his master praying for his liberty. The jury decided that there was "no law in the Province to hold a man to serve for life," and the slave of Caleb Dodge won the suit.

Felix Holbrook and other slaves presented a petition to the Massachusetts House of Representatives in 1773, asking to be set free and granted some unimproved lands where they might earn an honest living as freemen. Their petition was delayed consideration one year, and finally passed. But the English governors, Hutchinson and Gage, refused to sign it, because they perhaps thought it would " choke the channel of a commerce in human souls."

British Hatred to Negro freedom thus made itself plain to the New England slaves, and a few years later, when England fired her guns to subdue the revolution begun at Lexington, the slave population enlisted largely in the defence of the colonists. And thus the Negro slave by valor, patriotism and industry, began to loosen the chains of his own bondage in the Northern colonies.

PHILLIS WHEATLEY.

Before passing from the New England colonies it would be unfortunate to the readers of this book were they not made acquainted with the great and wonderful career of the young Negro slave who bore the above name. She came from Africa and was sold in a Boston slave market in the year 1761 to a kind lady who was a Mrs. Wheatley. As she sat with a crowd of slaves in the market, naked, save

a piece of cloth tied about the loins, her modest, intelligent bearing so attracted Mrs. Wheatley that

Phillis Wheatley

she selected her in preference to all the others. Her
selection proved a good one, for, with clean clothing
and careful attention, Phillis soon began to show a
great desire for learning.   Though only eight years
old, this young African, whose race all the learned
men said were incapable of culture, within little over
a year's time so mastered the English language as

to be able to read the most difficult parts of the
Bible intelligently. Her achievements in two or
three years drew the leading lights of Boston to
Mrs. Wheatley's house, and with them Phillis talked
and carried on correspondence concerning the popular topics of the day. Everybody either knew or
knew of Phillis. She became skilled in Latin and
translated one of Ovid's stories, which was published
largely in English magazines. She published many
poems in English, one of which was addressed to
General George Washington. He sent her the following letter in reply, which shows that Washington
was as great in heart as in war :

CAMBRIDGE, 28 February, 1776.

" *Miss Phillis :*—Your favor of the 26th October
did not reach my hands till the middle of December.
. . . . I thank you most sincerely for your polite
notice of me in the elegant lines you enclosed ; and
however undeserving I may be of such encomium and
panegyric, the style and manner exhibit a striking
proof of your poetical talents, in honor of which, and
as a tribute justly due to you, I would have published the poem, had I not been apprehensive that,
while I only meant to give the world this new instance of your genius, I might have incurred the imputation of vanity. This and nothing else, determined me not to give it place in the public prints.

"If you should ever come to Cambridge, or near
headquarters, I shall be happy to see a person **so**
favored by the Muses, and to whom Nature has been
so liberal and beneficent in her dispensations. I
am with great respect,

"Your humble servant,

"George Washington."

— *Williams.*

Phillis was emancipated at the age of twenty-one.
Soon after that her health failed and she was sent
to Europe, where she created even a greater sensation than in America. Men and women in the very
highest stations of the Old World were wonder-
struck, and industriously attentive to this humble
born African girl. While Phillis was away Mrs.
Wheatley became seriously ill and her daily long-
ings were to see "her Phillis," to whom she was so
much devoted. It is related that she would often
turn on her sick-couch and exclaim, "See! Look at
my Phillis! Does she not seem as though she would
speak to me?" Phillis was sent for to come, and in
response to the multitude of kindnesses done her by
Mrs. Wheatley, she hastened to her bed-side where
she arrived just before Mrs. Wheatley died, and
"shortly had time to close her sightless eyes."

Mr. Wheatley, after the death of his wife, married
again and settled in England. Phillis being thus

left alone also married. Her husband was named Peters. He, far inferior to her in most every way, and becoming jealous of the favors shown her by the best of society, became very cruel. Phillis did not long survive his harsh treatment, and she died "greatly beloved" and mourned on two continents, December 5, 1784, at the age of 31.

Thus passed away one of the brightest of the race, whose life was as pure as a crystal and devoted to the most beautiful in poetry, letters and religion, and exemplifies the capabilities of the race.

She composed this verse:

> " 'Twas mercy brought me from my Pagan land,
> Taught my benighted soul to understand
> That there's a God—that there's a Saviour, too ;
> Once I redemption neither sought nor knew."

Contrary to the *Connecticut slaveholders' feigned* unbelief in the intellectual capacity of the Negro, and their assertions of his utter inferiority in all things, they early enacted the most rigid laws prohibiting the teaching of any Negro to read, bond or free, with a penalty of several hundred dollars for every such act. The following undeniable story is woven into the fabric of Connecticut's history, and tells a sad tale of the prejudice of her people against the Negro during the days of slavery there:

"**Prudence Crandall,** a young Quaker lady of

talent, was employed to teach a 'boarding and day-school.' While at her post of duty one day, Sarah Harris, whose father was a well-to-do colored farmer, applied for admission. Miss Crandall hesitated somewhat to admit her, but knowing the girl's respectability, her lady-like and modest deportment, for she was a member of the white people's church and well known to them, she finally told her yes. The girl came. Soon Miss Crandall was called upon by the patrons, announcing their disgust and loathing that their daughters should attend school with a 'nigger girl.' Miss Crandall protested, but to no avail. The white pupils were finally taken from the school. Miss Crandall then opened a school for colored ladies. She enrolled about twenty, but they were subjected to many outrageous insults. They were denied accommodation altogether in the village of Canterbury. Their well was filled up with trash, and all kinds of unpleasant and annoying acts were thrust upon them. The people felt determined that Canterbury should not have the disgrace of a colored school. No, not even the State of Connecticut. Miss Crandall sent to Brooklyn to some of her friends. They pleaded in her behalf privately, and went to a town meeting to speak for her, but were denied the privilege. Finally, the Legislature passed a law prohibiting colored schools in the State. From the advice of her friends and her own strong will, Miss Crandall continued to teach. She was arrested and her friends were sent for. They came, but would not be persuaded by the sheriff and other officers to stand her bond. The people saw the disgrace and felt ashamed to have it go down in history that she was put in jail. In agreement with Miss Crandall's wishes her friends still persisted, so about night she was put in jail, into a murderer's cell. The news flashed over the country, much to the Connecticut people's chagrin and disgrace. She had her trial—the court evaded giving a decision. She opened her school again, and an attempt was made to burn up the building while she and the pupils were there, but proved unsuccessful. One night about midnight they were aroused to find themselves besieged by persons with heavy iron bars and clubs breaking the windows and tearing things to pieces. It was then thought unwise to continue the school longer. So the doors were closed, and the poor girls, whose only offence was a manifestation for knowledge, were sent to their homes. This law, however, was repealed in 1838, after lasting five years.

CHAPTER V.

NEW HAMPSHIRE AND MARYLAND.

New Hampshire slaves were very few in number. The people of this colony saw the evils of slavery very early, and passed laws against their importation. Massachusetts was having so much trouble with her slaves that the New Hampshire people early made up their minds that, as a matter of business as well as of humanity, they had best not try to build up their colony by dealing in human flesh and blood.

Maryland was, up to 1630, a part of Virginia, and slavery there partook of the same features. Owing to the feeling existing in the colony between the Catholics, who planted it, and the Protestants, the slaves were treated better than in some other provinces. Yet their lot was a hard one at best. By law, a white person could kill a slave, and not suffer death; only pay a fine.

White Slaves existed in this colony, many of whom came as criminals from England. They, it seems, were chiefly domestic servants, while the **Negroes worked the tobacco** fields.

BENJAMIN BANNEKA, ASTRONOMER AND
MATHEMATICIAN.

Banneka was born in Maryland in the year 1731. An English woman named Molly Welsh, who came to Maryland as an emigrant, is said to have been his maternal grandmother. This woman was sold as a slave to pay her passage to this country on board an emigrant ship, and after serving out her term of slavery she bought two Negro slaves herself. These slaves were men of extraordinary powers, both of mind and body. One of them, said to be the son of an African king, was set free by her, and she soon married him. There were four children, and one of them, named Mary, married a native African, Robert Banneka, who was the father of Benjamin.

The School Days of young Benjamin were spent in a "pay school," where some colored children were admitted. The short while that Benjamin was there he learned to love his books, and when the other children played he was studying. He was very attentive to his duties on his father's farm, and when through with his task of caring for the horses and cows, he would spend his leisure hours in reading books and papers on the topics of the day.

The Post-Office was the famous gathering place in those days, and there it was that young Benjamin was accustomed to go. He met many of the leading people of the community, and fluently discussed with them difficult questions. He could answer almost any problem put to him in mathematics, and became known throughout the colonies as a genius. Many of his answers to questions were beyond the reach of ordinary minds.

Messrs. Ellicott & Co., who built flour mills on the Patapsco River near Baltimore, very early discovered Banneka's genius, and Mr. George Ellicott allowed him the use of his library and astronomical instruments. The result of this was that Benjamin Banneka published his first almanac in the year 1792, said to be the first almanac published in America. Before that he had made numerous calculations in astronomy and constructed for himself a splendid clock that, unfortunately, was burned with his dwelling soon after his death.

Banneka's Reputation spread all over America and even to Europe. He drew to him the association of the best and most learned men of his country. His ability was a curiosity to everybody, and did much to establish the fact that the Negro of his time could master the arts and sciences. It is said that he was the master of five different languages, as well as a mathematical and astronomical genius.

He accompanied and assisted the commissioners who surveyed the District of Columbia.

He sent Mr Thomas Jefferson one of his alma-nacs, which Mr Jefferson prized so highly that he sent it to Paris, and wrote Mr. Banneka the following letter in reply   Along with Mr. Banneka's almanac to Mr. Jefferson he sent a letter pleading for better treatment of the people of African descent in the United States.

MR. JEFFERSON'S LETTER TO B. BANNEKA.

PHILADELFHIA, August 30, 1791.

"*Dear Sir*—I thank you sincerely for your letter of the 19th instant, and for the almanac it contained. Nobody wishes more than I do to see such proofs as you exhibit that Nature has given to our black brethren talents equal to those of the other colors of men, and that the appearance of a want of them is owing only to the degraded condition of their existence, both in Africa and America   I can add with truth, that no one wishes more ardently to see a good system commenced for raising the condition, both of their body and mind, to what it ought to be, as fast as the imbecility of their present existence, and other circumstances which cannot be neglected, will admit.   I have taken the liberty of sending your almanac to Monsieur de Cordorat, Secretary of the Academy of Sciences at Paris and member of the

Philanthropic Society, because I considered it a document to which your whole color had a right for their justification against the doubts which have been entertained of them.

"I am, with great esteem, sir,

"Your most obedient servant,

"Thos. Jefferson."

*Mr. Benjamin Banneka, near Ellicott's
Lower Mills, Baltimore County.*

The Personal Appearance of Mr. Banneka is drawn from the letters of those who wrote about him. A certain gentleman who met him at Ellicott's Mills gives this description : " Of black complexion, medium stature, of uncommonly soft and gentlemanly manners, and of pleasing colloquial powers."

Mr. Banneka died about the year 1804, very greatly mourned by the people of this country and Europe. He left two sisters, who, according to his request, turned over his books, papers, and astronomical calculations to Mr. Ellicott. There has been no greater mind in the possession of any American citizen than that of Benjamin Banneka. He stands out in history as one of those phenomenal characters whose achievements seem to be nothing short of miraculous.

Frances Ellen Watkins was another of Maryland's bright slaves. She distinguished herself as an anti-slavery lecturer in the Eastern States, and wrote a book entitled, " Poems and Miscellaneous Writings: By Frances Ellen Watkins." In that book was the following poem entitled " Ellen Harris:"

(1) Like a fawn from the arrow, startled and wild,
     A woman swept by me bearing a child;
     In her eye was the night of a settled despair,
     And her brow was overshadowed with anguish and care.

(2) She was nearing the river,—on reaching the brink
     She heeded no danger, she paused not to think !
     For she is a mother—her child is a slave,—
     And she'll give him his freedom or find him a grave !

(3) But she's free,—yes, free from the land where the slave
     From the hand of oppression must rest in the grave ;
     Where bondage and torture, where scourges and chains,
     Have placed on our banner indelible stains.

(4) The blood-hounds have missed the scent of her way ;
     The hunter is rifled and foiled of his prey ;
     Fierce jargon and cursing, with clanking of chains,
     Make sounds of strange discord on Liberty's plains.

(5) With the rapture of love and fulness of bliss,
     She placed on his brow a mother's fond kiss,—
     Oh ! poverty, danger, and death she can brave,
     For the child of her love is no longer a slave !

CHAPTER VI.

DELAWARE AND PENNSYLVANIA.

Delaware was settled, as you will remember, by the Swedes and Danes, in 1639. They were a simple, contented, and religious people. It is recorded that they had a law very early in their history declaring it was " not lawful to buy and keep slaves." It is very evident, though, that later on in the history of the colony slaves were held, and their condition was the same as in New York. While the north of the colony was perhaps fully in sympathy with slavery, the western part was influenced by the religious sentiment of the *Quakers in Pennsylvania.*

The Friends of Pennsylvania were opposed to slavery, and although slavery was tolerated by law, the way was left open for their education and religious training. In 1688, Francis Daniel Pastorious* addressed a memorial to the Friends of Germantown. His was said to be the first protest against slavery made by any of the churches of America. He believed that " slave and slave-owner should be equal at the Master's feet."

William Penn showed himself friendly to the slaves.

* Williams.

CHAPTER VII.

NORTH CAROLINA.

THIS colony, in geographical position, lies between South Carolina and Virginia. While it held slaves, it may be justly said its position on this great question was not so burdensome to the slave as the other Southern colonies, and even to the present time the Negroes and whites of this State seem to enjoy the most harmonious relations. The slave laws of this State gave absolute dominion of the master over the servant, but allowed him to join the churches from the first. Large communities of free Negroes lived in this State prior to the civil war, and, as late as the year 1835, could vote. They had some rights of citizenship and many of them became men of note.

Prior to the Civil War there were schools for these free people. Some of them owned slaves themselves. In this colony the slaves were worked, as a rule, on small farms, and there was a close relation established between master and slave, which bore its fruits in somewhat milder treatment than was customary in colonies where the slave lived on

large cotton plantations governed by cruel overseers, some of whom were imported from the North.

The Eastern Section of North Carolina was
thickly peopled with slaves, and some landlords
owned as many as two thousand.

The increase and surplusage of the slave population in this State was sold to the more Southern
colonies, where they were used on the cotton plantations.

A NORTH CAROLINA SLAVE POET.

George M. Horton was his name. He was the
slave of James M. Horton, of Chatham county, N.
C. Several of his special poems were published in
the Raleigh *Register*. In 1829, A. M. Gales, of this
State, afterwards of the firm of Gales and Seaton,
Washington, D. C., published a volume of the slave
Horton's poems, which excited the wonder and admiration of the best men in this country. His
poems reached Boston, where they were much talked
of, and used as an argument against slavery. Hor
ton, at the time his volume was published, could
read but not write, and was, therefore, compelled to
dictate his productions to some one who wrote them
down for him. He afterwards learned to write.
He seemed to have concealed all his achievements
from his master, who knew nothing of his slave's
ability except what others told him. He simply

knew George as a field hand, which work he did faithfully and honestly, and wrote his poetry too. Though a slave, his was a noble soul inspired with the Muse from above. The Raleigh *Register* said of him, July 2d, 1829: "That his heart has felt deeply and sensitively in this lowest possible condition of human nature (meaning slavery) will be easily believed, and is impressively confirmed by one of his stanzas, viz. :

> "Come, melting pity from afar,
> And break this vast, enormous bar
> Between a wretch and thee;
> Purchase a few short days of time,
> And bid a vassal soar sublime
> On wings of Liberty."

CHAPTER VIII.

SOUTH CAROLINA.

CHARTERS for the settlement of North and South Carolina were obtained at the same time—1663. Slavery commenced with the colony. Owing to the peculiar fitness of the soil for the production of rice and cotton, slave labor was in great demand. White labor failed, and the colony was marvellously prosperous under the slave system. Negroes were imported from Africa by the thousands. Their labor proved very productive, and here it was that the slave code reached its maximum of harshness.

A Negro Regiment in the service of Spain was doing duty in Florida, and through it the Spanish, who were at dagger's ends with the British colonies, sent out spies who offered inducements to such of the South Carolina slaves as would run away and join them. Many slaves ran away. Very rigid and extreme laws were passed to prevent slaves from running away, such as branding, and cutting the "ham-string" of the leg.

A Riot followed the continued cruel treatment of the slaves under the runaway code; 1748 is said

to have been the year in which a crowd of slaves
assembled in the village of Stono, slew the guards
at the arsenal and secured the ammunition there.
They then marched to the homes of several leading
men whom they murdered, together with their wives
and children. The slaves captured considerable
rum in their plundering expedition, and having indulged very freely, stopped for a frolic, and in the
midst of their hilarity were captured by the whites,
and thus ended the riot.

The Discontent of the Slaves grew, however,
in spite of the speedy ending of this attempt at insurrection. Cruel and inhuman treatment was bearing its fruits in a universal dissatisfaction of the
slaves, and in South Carolina, as in Massachusetts,
it began to be a serious question as to what side the
slaves would take in the war of the coming Revolu
tion. England offered freedom and money to slaves
who would join her army. The people of South
Carolina did not wait long before they allowed the
Negroes to enlist in defence of the colonies, and
highly complimented their valor. If a slave killed
a Briton he was emancipated; if he were taken
prisoner and escaped back into the Province, he was
also set free.

CHAPTER IX.

GEORGIA.

FROM the time of its settlement in 1732 till 1750 this colony held no slaves. Many of the inhabitants were anxious for the introduction of slaves, and when the condition of the colony finally became hopeless they sent many long petitions to the Trustees, stating that "*the one thing needful*" for their prosperity was Negroes. It was a long time before the Trustees would give their consent; they said that the colony of Georgia was designed to be a protection to South Carolina and the other more Northern colonies against the Spanish, who were then occupying Florida, and if the colonists had to control slaves it would weaken their power to defend themselves. Finally, owing to the hopeless condition of the Georgia colony, the Trustees yielded. Slaves were introduced in large numbers.

Prosperity came with the slaves, and, as in the case of Virginia, the colony of Georgia took a fresh start and began to prosper. White labor proved a failure. It was the honest and faithful toil of the Negro that turned the richness of Georgia's soil into

English gold, built cities and created large estates, gilded mansions furnished with gold and silver plate.*

Oglethorpe Planned the Georgia colony as a home for Englishmen who had failed in business and were imprisoned for their debts. These English people were out of place in the wild woods of America, and continued a failure in America, as well as in England, until the toiling but "heathen" African came to their aid.

Cotton Plantations were numerous in Georgia under the slave system. The slave-owners had large estates, numbering thousands of acres in many cases. The slaves were experts in the culture of cotton. The climate was adapted to sugar-cane and rice, both of which were raised in abundance.

---

* The famous minister, George Whitfield, referring to his plantation in this colony, said: "Upward of five thousand pounds have been expended in the undertaking, and yet very little proficiency made in the cultivation of my tract of land, and that entirely owing to the necessity I lay under of making use of white hands. Had a Negro been allowed I should now have had a sufficiency to support a great many orphans, without expending above half the sum which had been laid out." He purchased a plantation in South Carolina, where slavery existed, and speaks of it thus: "Blessed be God! This plantation has succeeded; and though at present I have only eight working hands, yet, in all probability, there will be more raised in one year, and without a quarter of the expense, than has been produced at Bethesda for several years past. This confirms me in the opinion I have entertained for a long time, that *Georgia never can or will be a flourishing province without Negroes are allowed.*"

BLOUNT'S FORT.

This fortification, erected by some of the armies during the early colonial wars, had been abandoned. It lies on the west bank of the Apalachicola river in Florida, forty miles from the Georgia line. Negro refugees from Georgia fled into the everglades of Florida as a hiding-place during the war of the Revolution. In these swamps they remained for forty years successfully baffling all attempts to re-enslave them. Many of those who planned the escape at first were now dead, and their children had grown up to hate the lash and love liberty. Their parents had taught them that to die in the swamps with liberty was better than to feast as a bondman and a slave. When Blount's Fort was abandoned and taken possession of by these children of the swamp, there were three hundred and eleven of them, out of which not more than twenty had ever been slaves. They were joined by other slaves who ran away as chance permitted. The neighboring slave-holders attempted to capture these people but failed. They finally called on the President of the United States for aid. General Jackson, then commander of the Southern militia, delegated Lieutenant Colonel Clinch to take the fort and reduce these people to slavery again. His sympathies being with the refugees, he marched to the fort and returned, reporting that " the fortification **was not** accessible by land."

Commodore Patterson next received orders. He commanded the American fleet, then lying in Mobile Bay. A " sub-order was given instantly to Lieutenant Loomis to ascend the Apalachicola river with two gun-boats, to seize the people in Blount's Fort, deliver them to their owners, and destroy the fort." At early dawn on the morning of September the 17th, 1816, the two boats, with full sail catching a gentle breeze, moved up the river towards the fort. They lowered a boat on their arrival and twelve men went ashore. They were met at the water's edge and asked their errand by a number of the leading men of the fort. Lieutenant Loomis informed them that he came to destroy the fort and turn over its inmates to the "slave-holders, then on board the gun-boat, who claimed them as fugitive slaves." The demand was rejected. The colored men returned to the fort and informed the inmates. Great consternation prevailed. The women were much distressed, but amid the confusion and excitement there appeared an aged father whose back bore the print of the lash, and whose shoulder bore the brand of his master. He assured the people that the fort could not be taken, and ended his speech with these patriotic words : "Give me liberty, or give me death." The shout went up from the

4

entire fort as from one man, and they prepared to face the enemy.

The Gun-boats Soon Opened Fire. For several hours they buried balls in the earthen walls and injured no one. Bombs were then fired. These had more effect, as there was no shelter from them. Mothers were more careful to hug their young babies closer to their bosoms. All this seemed little more than sport for the inmates of the fort, who saw nothing but a joke in it after shelter had been found.

Lieutenant Loomis saw his failure. He had a consultation, and it was agreed to fire "hot shot at the magazine." So the furnaces were heated and the fiery flames began to whizz through the air. This last stroke was effectual; the hot shot set the magazine on fire, and a terrible explosion covered the entire place with *débris.* Many were instantly killed by the falling earth and timbers. The mangled limbs of mothers and babies lay side by side. It was now dark. Fifteen persons in the fort had survived the explosion. The sixty sailors and officers now entered, trampling over the wounded and dying, and took these fifteen refugees in handcuffs and ropes back to the boats. The dead, wounded and dying were left.

As the two boats moved away from this scene of carnage the sight weakened the veteran sailors on board the boats, and when the officers retired these weather-worn sailor veterans "gathered before the mast, and loud and bitter were the curses uttered against slavery and against the officers of the government who had thus constrained them to murder innocent women and helpless children, merely for their love of liberty."

The Dead Remained unburied in the fort. The wounded and dying were not cared for, and all were left as fat prey for vultures to feast upon. For fifty years afterward the bones of these brave people lay bleaching in the sun. Twenty years after the murder a Representative in Congress from one of the free States introduced a bill giving a gratuity to the perpetrators of this crime. The bill passed both houses.

———————

Having briefly considered the establishment of slavery in the colonies, where the Negro slave was employed in every menial occupation, and where he accepted the conditions imposed upon him with a full knowledge of the wrong done, but still jubilant with songs of hope for deliverance, and trust in God, whose promises are many to the faithful, let us turn to

The War of the Revolution, which soon came

on ; and in it Providence no doubt designed an opportunity for the race to loosen the rivets in the chains that bound them. They made good use of this opportunity.

CHAPTER X.

HABITS AND CUSTOMS OF THE SOUTHERN COLONIES.

Barnes gives the following account of the habits and customs of the Southern colonies during the days of slavery:

"**The Southern Colonists** differed widely from the Northern in habits and style of living. In place of thickly-settled towns and villages, they had large plantations, and were surrounded by a numerous household of servants. The Negro quarters formed a hamlet apart, with its gardens and poultry yards. An estate in those days was a little empire. The planter had among his slaves men of every trade, and they made most of the articles needed for common use upon the plantation. There were large sheds for curing tobacco, and mills for grinding corn and wheat. The tobacco was put up and consigned directly to England. The flour of the Mount Vernon estate was packed under the eye of Washington himself, and we are told that barrels of flour bearing his brand passed in the West India market without inspection.

"**Up the Ashley and Cooper** (near Charleston) were the remains of the only *bona fide* nobility ever established on our soil. There the descendants of the Landgraves, who received their title in accordance with Locke's grand model, occupied their manorial dwellings. Along the banks of the James and Rappahannock the plantation often passed from father to son, according to the law of entail.

"The heads of these great Southern families lived like lords, keeping their packs of choice hunting dogs, and their stables of blooded horses, and rolling to church or town in their coach of six, with outriders on horseback. Their spacious mansions were sometimes built of imported brick. Within, the grand staircases, the mantels, and the wainscot, reaching in a quaint fashion from floor to ceiling, were of mahogany elaborately carved and paneled. The sideboards shone with gold and silver plate and the tables were loaded with the luxuries of the Old World. Negro servants thronged about, ready to perform every task.

"**All labor was done by Slaves**, it being considered degrading for a white man to work. Even the superintendence of the plantation and slaves was generally committed to overseers, while the master dispensed a generous hospitality, and occupied himself with social and political life."

SLAVERY INTRODUCED IN THE COLONIES.

In Virginia, the last of August, 1619.

In New York, 1628.

In Massachusetts, 1637

In Maryland, 1634.

In Delaware, 1636.

In Connecticut, between 1631 and 1636.

In Rhode Island from the beginning, 1647.

New Jersey, not known; as early though as in New Netherland.

South Carolina and North Carolina from the earliest days of existence.

In New Hampshire, slavery existed from the beginning.

Pennsylvania doubtful.

CHAPTER XI.

NEGRO SOLDIERS IN REVOLUTIONARY TIMES.

Objections to Enlisting Negroes caused much discussion at the beginning of the Revolutionary war. The Northern colonies partially favored their enlistment because they knew of their bravery, and rightly reasoned that if the Negroes were not allowed to enlist in the Colonial army, where their sympathies were, they would accept the propositions of the British, who promised freedom to every slave who would desert his master and join the English army.

Lord Dunmore, Governor of Virginia, and the other British leaders, saw a good chance to weaken the strength of the colonies by offering freedom to the slaves if they would fight for England. They knew that the slaves would be used to throw up fortifications, do fatigue duties, and raise the provisions necessary to support the Colonial army. So Lord Dunmore issued a proclamation offering freedom to all slaves who would join his army. As the result of this, Thomas Jefferson is quoted as saying that 30,000 Negroes from Virginia alone joined the British ranks.

The Americans became fearful of the results that were sure to follow the plans of Lord Dunmore. Sentiment began to change in the Negro's favor; the newspapers were filled with kind words for the slaves, trying to convince them that the British Government had forced slavery upon the colonies against their will, and that their best interests were centred in the triumph of the Colonial army. A part of an article in one paper, headed " Caution to the Negro," read thus: "Can it, then, be supposed that the Negroes will be better used by the English, who have always encouraged and upheld this slavery, than by their present masters, who pity their condition; who wish in general to make it as easy and comfortable as possible, and who would, were it in their power, or were they permitted, not only prevent any more Negroes from losing their freedom, but restore it to such as have already unhappily lost it. . . . . They will send the Negroes to the West Indies where every year they sell many thousands of their miserable brethren. Be not tempted, ye Negroes, to ruin yourselves by this proclamation!" The colonies finally allowed the enlistment of Negroes, their masters being paid for them out of the public treasury. Those slaves who had already joined the British were offered pardon if they would escape and return, and a severe punishment was to be inflicted on those who left the colony if they were caught.

To Offset the Plans of Lord Dunmore, the Americans proposed to organize a Negro army, to be commanded by the brave Colonel Laurens ; and on this subject the following letter was addressed to John Jay, President of Congress, by the renowned Alexander Hamilton. This letter also shows in what esteem the Negro slave of America was held by men of note:

"HEADQUARTERS, March 14, 1779.

" *To. John Jay.*

"DEAR SIR:—Col. Laurens, who will have the honor of delivering you this letter, is on his way to South Carolina on a project which I think, in the present situation of affairs there, is a very good one, and deserves every kind of support and encouragement. This is, to raise two, or three, or four battalions of Negroes, with the assistance of the government of that State, by contributions from the owners in proportion to the number they possess. If you think proper to enter upon the subject with him, he will give you a detail of his plan. He wishes to have it recommended by Congress and the State, and, as an inducement, they should engage to take those battalions into Continental pay.

"It appears to me that an experiment of this kind, in the present state of Southern affairs, is the most rational that can be adopted, and promises very important advantages. Indeed, I hardly see how a sufficient force can be collected in that quarter without it, and the enemy's operations are growing infinitely more serious and formidable. I have not the least doubt that the Negroes will make very excellent soldiers with proper management, and I will venture to pronounce that they cannot be put in better hands than those of Mr. Laurens. He has all the zeal, intelligence, enterprise, and every other qualification necessary to succeed in such an under-taking. It is a maxim with some great military judges that, "with sensible officers, soldiers can hardly be too stupid;" and, on this principle, it is thought that the Russians would make the best troops in the world if they were under other officers than their own. I mention this, because I hear it frequently objected to the scheme of embodying Negroes, that they are too stupid to make soldiers. This is so far from appearing, to me, a valid objection, that I think their want of cultivation (for their natural faculties are probably as good as ours), joined to that habit of subordination from a life of servitude, will make them sooner become soldiers than our white inhabitants. Let officers be men of sense and sentiment, and the nearer the soldiers approach to machines perhaps the better.

"I foresee that this project will have to combat much opposition from prejudice and self-interest. The contempt we have been taught to entertain for the blacks makes us fancy many things that are founded neither in reason nor experience, and an unwillingness to part with property of so valuable a kind will furnish a thousand arguments to show the impracticability or pernicious tendency of a scheme which requires such a sacrifice. But it should be considered that if we do not make use of them in this way the enemy probably will, and that the best way to counteract the temptations they hold out will be to offer them ourselves. An essential part of the plan is to give them their freedom with their muskets. This will secure their fidelity, animate their courage, and, I believe, will have a good influence upon those who remain by opening a door to their emancipation. This circumstance, I confess, has no small weight in inducing me to wish the success of the project, for the dictates of humanity and true policy equally interest me in favor of this unfortunate class of men. With the truest respect and esteem, I am, sir,

> "Your most obedient servant,
>> "ALEX. HAMILTON."

George Washington, James Madison, and the ontinental Congress gave their consent to the plan of Col. Laurens, and recommended it to the Southern Colonies. It was resolved by Congress to compensate the master for the slaves used by Col. Laurens at the rate of $1000 apiece for each "able-bodied Negro man of standard size, not exceeding thirty-five years of age, who shall be so enlisted and pass muster. That no pay be allowed to the said Negroes, but that they be clothed and subsisted at the expense of the United States; that every Negro who shall well and faithfully serve as a soldier to the end of the present war, and shall then return his arms, shall be emancipated and receive the sum of fifty dollars."

Congress commissioned Col. Laurens to carry out this plan. "He repaired to South Carolina and threw all his energies into his noble mission." The people of the States of Georgia and South Carolina refused to co-operate with him. It was difficult to get white troops to enlist. The Tories, who opposed the war against England, were very strong in several of the Southern colonies.

A Letter from General Washington will help us to understand the condition of affairs in South Carolina and Georgia. He wrote to Col. Laurens as follows: "I must confess that I am not at all astonished at the failure of your plan. That spirit of freedom which, at the commencement of this contest, would have gladly sacrificed everything to the attainment of its object, has long since subsided, and every selfish passion has taken its place. It is not the public but private interest which influences the generality of mankind, nor can the Americans any longer boast an exception. Under these circumstances it would rather have been surprising if you had succeeded, nor will you, I fear, have better success in Georgia."

Col. Laurens was killed in battle, but he had not entirely abandoned his plan of enlisting the slaves. But in spite of the recommendations of Congress, he could not succeed, for the States of South Carolina and Georgia coveted their slaves too much to allow this entering wedge to their ultimate freedom. Had his plan been carried out, slavery would probably have been abolished as soon at the South as at the North. The Negroes who would have come out of the war of the Revolution would have set themselves to work to relieve the condition of their brethren in shackles.

Connecticut Failed to endorse the enlistment of Negroes by its Legislature, but Mr. Williams in his history gives the roster of a company of Negroes in that State, numbering fifty-seven, with David Humphreys, Captain. White officers refused to serve in the company. David Humphreys continued at the head of this force until the war closed.

CHAPTER XII.

NEGRO HEROES OF THE REVOLUTION.

Among Those whose blood was first shed for
the cause of American liberty was the runaway slave,
Crispus Attucks. Having escaped from his master,
William Brown, of Framingham, Massachusetts, at
the age of twenty-seven, being then six feet two
inches high, with "short, curled hair," he made his
way to Boston. His master in 1750 offered a
reward of ten pounds for him, but Crispus was not
found. When next heard from he turns up in the
streets of Boston.

THE LEADER WHO FELL IN THE FAMOUS BOSTON
MASSACRE.

Attucks had no doubt been listening to the fiery
eloquence of the patriots of those burning times.
The words of the eloquent Otis had kindled his soul,
and though a runaway slave, his patriotism was so
deep that he it was who sacrificed his life *first* on the
altar of American Liberty.

General Gage, the English commander, had
taken possession of Boston. Under the British flag

Crispus Attucks at the Boston Massacre.

gaily dressed soldiers marched the streets of Boston as through a conquered city; their every act was an insult to the inhabitants. Finally, on March 5, 1770, Crispus Attucks, at the head of a crowd of citizens, resolved no longer to be insulted, and determining to resist any invasion of their rights as citizens, a fight soon ensued on the street. The troops were ordered to fire on the "mob," and Attucks fell, the first one, with three others, Caldwell, Gray, and Maverick. The town bell was rung, the alarm given and citizens from the country ran into Boston, where the greatest excitement prevailed.

The Burial of Attucks, the only unknown dead, was from Faneuil Hall. The funeral procession was enormous, and many of the best citizens of Boston readily followed this former slave and unknown hero to an honored grave. Many orators spoke in the highest terms of Crispus Attucks. A verse mentioning him reads thus:

> " Long as in freedom's cause the wise contend,
>   Dear to your country shall your fame extend ;
>   While to the world the lettered stone shall tell
>   Where Caldwell, Attucks, Gray and Maverick fell."

Peter Salem shoots Major Pitcairn at Bunker Hill.

Bunker Hill was the scene of a brave deed by a Negro soldier. Major Pitcairn was commander of the British forces there. The battle was fierce; victory seemed sure to the English, when Pitcairn mounted an eminence, shouting triumphantly, "The day is ours." At this moment the Americans stood as if dumfounded, when suddenly, with the leap of a tiger, there rushed forth *Peter Salem*, who fired directly at the officer's breast and killed him. Salem was said to have been a slave, of Framingham, Massachusetts. General Warren, who was killed in this battle, greatly eulogized Crispus Attucks for his bravery in Boston, and had he not been stricken down so soon, Peter Salem would doubtless also have received high encomiums from his eloquent lips.

Five Thousand Negroes are said to have fought on the side of the colonies during the Revolution. Most of them were from the northern colonies. There were, possibly, 50,000 Negroes enlisted on the side of Great Britain, and 30,000 of these were from Virginia.

SOME INDIVIDUALS OF REVOLUTIONARY TIMES.

Primus Hall, was body-servant of Colonel Pickering in Massachusetts. General Washington was quite intimate with the Colonel and paid him many visits. On one occasion, Washington continued his visit till a late hour, and being assured by Primus that there were blankets enough to accommodate him, he resolved to spend the night in the Colonel's quarters. Accordingly two beds of straw were made down, and Washington and Colonel Pickering retired, leaving Primus engaged about the tent. Late in the night General Washington awoke, and seeing Primus sitting on a box nodding, rose up in his bed and said : " Primus, what did you mean by saying that you had blankets enough ? Have you given up your blanket and straw to me, that I may sleep comfortably while you are obliged to sit through the night?" "It's nothing," said Primus; " don't trouble yourself about me, General, but go to sleep again. No matter about me; I sleep very good." "But it is matter; it is matter," replied Washington, earnestly. "I cannot do it, Primus. If either is to sit up, I will. But I think there is no need of either sitting up. The blanket is wide enough for two; come and lie down here with me." "O, no, General," said Primus; "let me sit here; I'll do very well on the box." Washington said, "I say, come and lie down here! There is room for both, and I insist upon it." And, as he spoke, he threw up the blanket and moved to one side of the straw. Primus hesitated, but Washington continuing to insist, Primus finally prepared himself and laid down by Washington, and on the same straw, and under the same blanket, where the General and the Negro servant slept till morning.

Washington is said to have been out walking one day in company with some distinguished gentlemen, and during the walk he met an old colored man, who very politely tipped his hat and spoke to the General. Washington, in turn, took off his hat to the colored man, on seeing which one of the company, in a jesting manner, inquired of the General if he usually took off his hat to Negroes. Whereupon Washington replied: "Politeness is cheap, and I never allow any one to be more polite to me than I to him."

Brave Colored Artilleryman.

Judge Story gives an account of a colored artilleryman who was in charge of a cannon with a
white soldier at Bunker Hill. He had one arm so
badly wounded he could not use it. He suggested
to the white soldier that he change sides so as to
use the other arm. He did this; and while thus
laboring under pain and loss of blood, a shot came
which killed him.

Prince ―――― appears in the attempt to capture
General Prescott, of the Royal army, stationed at
Newport, R. I. General Lee, of the American forces,
was held as a prisoner by the British, and it was
designed to capture Prescott so as to be able to
give him in exchange for Lee. Colonel Barton
planned the scheme, and set out to Prescott's sleep-

ing apartments in the night.   Prince followed the
lead of Colonel Barton to the door.   There the sentinel was seized with his bayonet at the Colonel's
breast, and ordered to be silent on pain of death,
when Prince came forward and with two strokes at
the door with his head it came open.   Prescott was
seized by Prince while in bed and made a prisoner.
Colonel Barton was presented an elegant sword for
this brave exploit which Prince achieved.

Prince Whipple appears, as a body-guard, on
the picture entitled "Washington Crossing the Delaware."

L. LATHAM.

New London, Connecticut, was taken by the
British under command of Arnold, the traitor, in
1781.   The American troops retreated to Fort Gro
ton, where the American commander Ledyard was
in command.   The British came up and overcame
the Americans after a bold resistance.   The British
officer vainly strode into the ramparts and said,
"Who commands this fort?" Ledyard replied, "I
once did; you do now," handing the Briton his
sword at the same time, which he took and ran
through Ledyard up to the hilt.   L. Latham, a Negro slave, stood near the American.   *Scarcely had
the British officer's* hand left the murderous hilt when
Latham run him through with his bayonet.   The

enemy rushed on him, and after a most daring fight he fell, not till pierced by *thirty-three* bayonets. **L.** Latham had been left at home by his master to care for the stock when the latter left to help defend the fort; but as soon as he could unhitch his team he too made haste to the scene of the fray, and the above bold deed shows how deeply he felt moved to give his life in defence of his country.

John Freeman pinned Major Montgomery to the ground while he was being lifted upon the walls of Fort Griswold.

Samuel Charlton was in the battle of Monmouth and several others. Washington complimented him for his bravery. He returned to his master in New Jersey after the war, and at his master's death Charlton, with the other slaves, was set free and given a pension during his life.

James Armistead acted as scout for LaFayette in the Virginia campaign. He returned to his master after the surrender of Cornwallis and was set free by a special act of the Virginia Legislature.

Negro Soldiers in the North enlisted with the colonies so that they might thus get their freedom from their Northern masters, while Negro soldiers in the South enlisted with the British, who promised freedom to all who would join their ranks.

Did the Negro Soldiers get their freedom after the war of the Revolution was over? We may say yes, so far as the Northern colonies are concerned, but not without much opposition in the courts and legislatures. *Virginia* also passed an act in 1783 emancipating the slaves who had fought in the Revolution. Many individual slaves were emancipated by special acts of the legislatures for their courage and bravery.

George Washington set his slaves free by his will, and many slave-owners did the same.

The slaves who joined the British army were subjected to all sorts of horrors. Thousands died with small-pox and other contagious diseases. A great number were sent to the West Indies in exchange "for rum, sugar, coffee and fruit."

LAFAYETTE AND KOSCIUSKO.

LaFayette, the brilliant young Frenchman, and Kosciusko, the generous Pole, volunteered their services in behalf of freedom for the Americans during the Revolution. They fought, though, for the freedom of all Americans. LaFayette said in a letter to a Mr. Clarkson: "I would never have drawn my sword in the cause of America, if I could have conceived that thereby I was founding a land of slavery."

While Visiting America in 1825, he expressed a warm desire to see some of the many colored sol diers whom he "remembered as participating with him in various skirmishes." He believed in freedom to all men, and to put in practice his anti-slavery ideas he bought a plantation in French Guiana. There he collected all the "whips and other instruments of torture and punishment, and made a bonfire of them in the presence of the assembled slaves."

He Gave One Day in each week to the slaves, and as soon as one could earn enough he might purchase another day, and so on until he gained his freedom.

Kosciusko Expressed great sorrow to learn that the colored men who served in the Revolution were not thereby to gain their freedom. He left $20,000 in the hands of Thomas Jefferson, to be used in educating colored children.

CHAPTER XIII.

THE WAR OF 1812.

THE War of the Revolution ended in 1781 at Yorktown. Many of the brave Negroes who shed their blood and helped to win America's liberty from England were, as soon as the war closed, put back into bondage. They were in the "Land of the Free," but themselves slaves. Other troubles arose very soon between England and America. England still kept standing armies in America, and claimed the right to search American vessels for British sailors who had deserted. They often took off American seamen.

One Negro and Two White sailors were taken from the American man-of-war "Chesapeake" after she had been fired upon. Canada gave arms to and incited the Indians in the Northwest against the Americans. Finally, in 1812, war was declared, during Madison's administration.

Negro Troops were very much needed, as the Americans had a very poor navy, and England, having whipped the French, was now ready to turn all her forces against America.

A Call for Volunteers from the Union was

issued, and many thousands of free Negroes an-swered the call. The slaves were not allowed to enlist in the militia. Gen. Jackson thus spoke to his colored troops :

"*To the Men of Color—Soldiers :* From the shores of Mobile I collected you to arms. I invited you to share in the perils and to divide the glory with your white countrymen. I expected much from you, for I was not uninformed of those qualities which must render you so formidable to an invading foe. I knew that you could endure hunger and thirst and all the hardships of war. I knew that you loved the land of your nativity, and that, like ourselves, you had to defend all that is most dear to man. *But you have surpassed all my hopes.* I have found in you, united to these qualities, that noble enthusiasm which impels to great deeds.

"Soldiers, the President of the United States shall be informed of your conduct on the present occasion, and the voice of the Representatives of the American nation shall applaud your valor as your General now praises your ardor. The enemy is near. His sails cover the lakes ; but the brave are united, and if he finds us contending among ourselves, it will be for the prize of valor, and fame, its noblest reward."

The Battle of New Orleans, we will remember, ended in defeat for the British. Over two thousand were lost to the British, while the American loss was seven killed and six wounded. There were over four hundred Negroes in this battle, and they occupied " no mean place and did no mean service." The British had a battalion of Negroes from the Island of San Domingo in this battle. The idea of fortifying the city with cotton is said to have been the suggestion of a slave who was a native African, and learned this mode of defence from the Arabs.

Mr. D. Lee Child, in a letter to a friend, states that the famous *cotton breast-works*, recognized the world over as a stroke of genius on the part of Gen. Jackson, was the suggestion of a colored man, a native African. He gives some data from a Portuguese manuscript to prove that this mode of defence is in practice among the native Africans, who thus defend their wives and children against the Arabs.

NEGROES IN THE NAVY OF 1812.

There seemed to be no discrimination against any class of citizens joining our navy; nor is there now. About one-fifth of the marines were Negroes. That they did valuable service is testified to by numerous commanders. Read what Commander Nathaniel Shaler of the " private armed " schooner " Governor Tompkins " says, in a letter dated—

"AT SEA, Jan. 1, 1813.

"My officers conducted themseives in a way that would have done honor to a more permanent service. . . . . The name of one of my poor fellows who was killed *ought to be registered in the book of fame*, and remembered with reverence as long as bravery is a virtue, He was a black man, by the name of *John Johnson.* A twenty-four pound shot struck him in the hip and took away all the lower part of his body. In this state the poor, brave fellow lay on the deck, and several times exclaimed to his shipmates, '*Fire away, my boys; no haul a color down !*' The other was a black man by the name of John Davis, and was struck in much the same way. He fell near me, and several times requested to be thrown overboard, saying he was only in the way of others. While America has such tars, she has little to fear from the tyrants of the ocean."

Captain Perry had command of the American fleet on Lake Erie. He objected to recruits sent him, and described them in a letter to Commodore Chauncey as "a motley set—blacks, soldiers and boys." Commodore Chauncey replied: "I regret that you are not pleased with the men sent you. . . . . I have yet to learn that the color of the skin, or the cut and trimmings of the coat, can affect a man's qualifications or usefulness. I have fifty blacks on board this ship, and many of them are among my best men."

Usher Parsons, Surgeon of the "Java," under Commodore Perry, wrote that the whites and blacks of his ship messed together, and there seemed to be no prejudice.

The End of the War of 1812 meant victory for America, and the Negro had scored a telling point in behalf of his recognition as an American citizen. But still many were in slavery.

Major Jeffreys, a "regular," during the engagement of Major-General Andrew Jackson at Mobile, mounted a horse and rallied the retreating troops to victory against the British, when the white commanders were forced to retire and defeat seemed certain. Gen. Jackson gave him the title of Major, which he bore till his death in Nashville, Tenn. He was much respected by all classes. On one occasion a white ruffian insulted him. Words ensued, and Major Jeffreys was forced to strike the white man in self-defence. For this, at the age of seventy years, this veteran, who had won a victory for his country on the battle-field, was ordered to be given "nine and thirty lashes with a raw hide." He did not recover from the effects of this treatment, and soon died of a broken heart.

Jordon Noble was among the colored veterans **of the War of 1812.** For a long time after the war he lived in New Orleans, where he was brought out on every great occasion to give enthusiasm. Jordon Noble's name appearing in connection with any great occasion was sufficient guarantee of a tremendous crowd. He was drummer to the First Regiment Louisiana Volunteers in the Mexican War of 1846, and led the attack against the British in the Battle of New Orleans under Jackson in 1814. He was known as the "matchless drummer."

CHAPTER XIV.

EFFORTS FOR FREEDOM.

The War of 1812 was now over. America remained at peace with other nations about thirty-
two years, when the Mexican war broke out in
1846. During this interval a war of words between
Americans themselves was waged ; and there were
heroes in this contest, many of them Negroes and
former slaves, and some of them women, who merit
equal rank with the brave heroes of former battles.

The Abolitionists who were opposed to slavery,
furnished many brave hearts and strong minds from
their ranks. Their work began very early in the
history of the colonies ; it continued with slow
growth for awhile, but nevertheless certain and
effectual. The Quakers of Pennsylvania were fore-
most in the work of abolition. They set nearly all
their slaves free. Anti-slavery societies were formed
in nearly all the Northern States.

Benjamin Lundy is mentioned as the earliest
leader of the Abolitionists. He published a paper
called *The Genius of Universal Emancipation.* He
visited nineteen States of the Union, travelled up-

waɪds of five thousand miles on foot, and more than twenty thousand in other ways, and held more than two hundred public meetings. Lundy's paper was not regarded as very dangerous to the institution of slavery; but the *Journal of the Times*, published first at Bennington, Vermont, in support of J. Q. Adams for the presidency, became the inveterate foe to slavery under the editorship of William Lloyd Garrison, who was mobbed in the streets of Boston, and imprisoned for libel in the city of Baltimore for denouncing the crew of the ship "Francis Todd," on board of which were many ill-treated slaves bound for the slave marts of New Orleans. Garrison and Lundy united in getting out *The Genius of Universal Emancipation* at Baltimore.

Arthur Tappan, before this, paid Garrison's fine, and the enemy to slavery commenced his war with more vigor and zeal than before. In 1831 *The Liberator* was first published by Garrison, and, as was his desire, it continued till "every slave in America was free."

A "Colored Man," James Forten, sent $50 among the first twenty-five subscriptions that came to *The Liberator*. Garrison thought it his duty to obey God rather than man, and he denounced the Constitution of the United States as being a "Covenant with death and an agreement with hell," because he held that it supported slavery.

The National Anti-Slavery Convention, white, was held in 1836; they had delegates from ten States, and 1006 anti-slavery societies existed in the different States.

The Free Colored People of the North also held an anti-slavery convention in 1831. Their first work was to get recognition from the white organizations, who shut them out. The "Anti-Slavery Free Women of America" organized in 1837, in New York. Mary S. Parker was President, Angelina E. Grimkie, Secretary.

Miss Sarah Forten addressed the following verses to her white sisters in behalf of co-operation :

> " We are thy sisters. God has truly said
> That of one blood all nations He has made.
> O Christian woman! in a Christian land,
> Canst thou unblushing read this great command ?
> Suffer the wrongs which wring our inmost heart,
> To draw one throb of pity on thy part?
> Our skins may differ, but from thee we claim
> A sister's privilege and a sister's name."

Soon after this, the free Negroes of the North acted together with the whites in the great fight against slavery. Negro orators told in eloquent style the sad story of the bondage of their race.

Frederick Douglass, once a slave in Maryland, electrified the whole country with his eloquence. He stood then, and now, as a living, breathing, convincing argument against the claim that the Negro's intellectual capacities fit him only for slavery. Mr. Douglass visited Europe and was received there with an ovation, for the cause of the slave had leaped across the Atlantic and touched a sympathetic chord in many a British heart.

Many Books were written by Negroes, as well as whites. Frederick Douglass wrote " My Bondage and My Freedom ;" Bishop Loguen, " As a Slave and as a Freeman ;" other works by Rev. Samuel R. Ward, Rev. Austin Stewart, Solomon Northorp, Dr. Wm. Wells Brown, and others. William Whipper edited an abolition paper, known as the *National Reformer*.

Uncle Tom's Cabin, by Mrs. Harriet Beecher Stowe, was the most read, and the most effectual work against slavery.

CHAPTER XV.

FREDERICK DOUGLASS.

THIS great man is well known to the world. He is a conspicuous representative of the talents and capabilities possessed by the colored race. Born a slave on a plantation in Maryland, he has gradually, by industry and patient labor, worked himself to the highest rank of honor, both in America and Europe. When Frederick Douglass speaks the world listens. He is as much quoted as any living American statesman.

The first ten years of Mr. Douglass' youth were spent on one of the many plantations of a rich planter named Lloyd, in the State of Maryland. He was separated from his mother, who only saw him at long intervals. He, with the other little slave boys, grew up from almost infancy in their tow shirts, with their ash-cake rations and frequent beatings, given them by a certain " old Aunt Kate," who had charge of the children on the plantation. In this wild way, young Fred was left to grow up as best he could among the rough farm hands and without a mother's care. He describes his mother

Frederick Douglass.

to have been a noble-looking woman, with the deepest of motherly affection and very fond of him, as shown by her running dangerous risks and often walking many long miles to see him.

At the age of ten years he was sent by his "Old Master" to live with his young mistress, in Baltimore, who was connected with the Lloyd family. This young lady became attached to him, and taught him to read. He learned to read the Bible and made such rapid progress that the young lady, feeling very proud of her work, told her husband. When he found it out he forbade her teaching him any further, saying it was unlawful, "could only lead to mischief," and, "if you give a nigger an inch he will take an ell." Nevertheless, Fred soon became proficient in reading, and he learned to write by the models in his young master's copy-book. He bought a book called the Columbian Orator, in which he found speeches from Sheridan, Lord Chatham, William Pitt and Fox. These he read many times and gained much mental help from them.

Finally, young Fred, whose mind now was enlightened, became so dissatisfied with his position as a slave that he grew morose and gloomy. His young mistress chided him for this conduct, and it finally became necessary to hire him out. He soon **found a good** opportunity and ran away to New

Bedford, Mass. Here he found employment and spent his leisure time in study. He read Scott's " Lady of the Lake," and there came across the name of Douglass, which he for the first time assumed. He attended church; was surprised to see the colored people transacting their own business. Some of the first money he earned in New Bedford was invested in a subscription to *The Liberator*. He was not long in coming to the front. His story of escape from slavery was told in the various churches, and the year 1841 found him on the stage before an anti-slavery convention at Nantucket. A tremendous crowd was present, and the wildest enthusiasm prevailed Mr. William Lloyd Garrison followed Mr. Douglass with a strong speech for the abolition of slavery. Mr. Douglass' career thus begun, continued; he spoke often and mightily for the cause of freedom. He became the leading orator of the time, and his presence was sufficient to draw a crowd in the bitterest pro slavery community.

Since freedom, Mr. Douglass has held several important positions under the National Government. He was once Recorder of Deeds in the District of Columbia, and is now Minister to the Haytian Republic.

CHAPTER XVI.

LIBERIA.

The Republic of Liberia was founded in 1816, by the American Colonization Society as a place of refuge and safety to the colored people of America who, before the abolition of slavery in the various States, had been set free by their masters, or, through industry, had purchased their liberty themselves. It is located on the west coast of Africa, south of Sierra Leone, and is very productive of rice, coffee, indigo, peanuts, arrowroot, sugar, pepper, logwood, palm-oil, and cotton.   Gold and other minerals are found in considerable quantities. The climate seems ill adapted to the American Negro.

Mr. Jehudi Ashmun was the pioneer in planting the colony, assisted by Lott Carey. The natives resisted the settlers, and for the first six years there were continual attempts to drive them out.   Mr. Ashmun's health finally failed, and he was compelled to leave the colony, now numbering 1200 free Americans, to themselves in this new and wild land. They shed bitter tears on his departure, some clinging even to his garments.   But, left to themselves, the Negroes did not lose all hope. They set about to found a goverment similar to that of the United States. They elected their first president, Joseph J. Roberts, organized a cabinet, established schools, made labor obligatory, and their flag is now recognized by the nations of Europe and the United States.

Its population is now over 20,000 Negroes who went from America, or their descendants. The influence of Liberia is exercised over a million of people along the West Coast of Africa. They speak English, and from them many tribes have learned our language and the arts of civilization. The United States has sent six Ministers to represent her at Monrovia, the Liberian capital, viz.: from North Carolina, Messrs. J. H. Smythe, Moses A. Hopkins, and E. E. Smith; from New York, Henry H. Garnet; Alexander Clark, of Iowa, and C. H. J. Taylor, of Kansas; Ernest Lyon, of Maryland, and Dr. W. D. Crum, of South Carolina. The exports of Liberia aggregate about three-quarters of a million dollars annually.

Success has thus far attended the country, though the climate, atmosphere, and the surroundings are most unfavorable and unstimulating. The fact that these colored people have succeeded shows what the race can do under favorable circumstances.

CHAPTER XVII.

NAT. TURNER AND OTHERS WHO "STRUCK ' FOR FREEDOM.

Nathaniel Turner is well remembered by many of the older people of Southampton, Virginia, as being the leader of the famous " Nat Turner Insurrection " of that county. He was an unusually bright child having learned to read and write with such skill and rapidity that his own people and the neighbors regarded him as a prodigy. It is said that his mother predicted that he would be a prophet in his presence one day, and he remembered her prediction till he grew older. Turner devoted himself to the study of the Scriptures and the condition of his people. He believed his lot was to set them free. He had visions of white and black spirits fighting in battle. He imagined a voice spoke thus to him in the vision: "Such is your luck ; such you are called to see; and let it come rough or smooth you must bear it." He thought, while laboring in the fields, " he discovered drops of blood on the corn, as though it were dew from heaven," and saw on the leaves of the trees pictures of men written in blood.

A Plan of Insurrection was devised in the month of February, 1831. Nat, together with four of his friends, Sam Edwards, Henry Porter, Nelson Williams, and Hark Travis, held a council of war, as it were, in some lonely, desolate spot in the woods, where they discussed the project of freeing the slaves. Nat said, in his speech, that his purpose was not to shed blood wantonly; but in order to arouse his brethren he believed it necessary to kill such of the whites as would be most likely to give them trouble. He, like John Brown, expected his slave brethren to join him.

The Fatal Stroke was given in the month of August, 1831. The first house visited was that of a Mr. Joseph Travis. While on the way, a slave from this plantation joined Nat's party. He was a giant of a man, athletic, quick, and "best man on the muscle in the county," and was known as "Will." The slaves were armed with axes and knives, and killed, indiscriminately, young and old, fifty-seven white persons, before they were killed or captured.

Several Artillery Companies from Richmond, seventy miles off, Petersburg, Norfolk, and Portsmouth, with one cavalry company, were ordered out to take Nat and his followers. In a hand-to-hand struggle Will fell. His last words were: "Bury my axe with me." Nat escaped with some others

to the swamps where he eluded the whites for nearly
three months.   After surrendering, he was brought
into court, and answered *Not Guilty* to the inquiry
of the judge.   The trial was gone through with.
Nat was convicted and condemned to die on the
gallows.   He received the sentence with total in-
difference, but made a prophecy that on the day
of his execution unusual occurrences would appear
in the heavens; the sun would be darkened and immense clouds would appear, and threatening lightning.   Many of the people believed it.   The sheriff
could find no one willing to cut the rope, but a
drunken sot, crazed by liquor, did the act for pay.
The day of execution, strange to say, as Nat had
prophesied, was one of stormy and gloomy aspect,
with terrible thunder, rain and lightning.   Nat kept
up his courage to the last, and his neck in the
noose, not a muscle quivered or a groan was uttered.
He was, undoubtedly, a wonderful character.   Know
ing as he did, the risk he ran, what an immense
courage he must have had to undertake this bold
adventure.   He was thus spoken of by a Mr.
Gray, who interviewed him : "It has been said that
he was ignorant and cowardly, and his purpose was
to murder and rob.   It is notorious that he was
never known to have a dollar in his life, to swear
an oath, or drink a drop of spirits.   He can read
and write, and for natural intelligence and quick-

ness of apprehension is surpassed by few men I have ever seen." *

Avery Watkins, a colored preacher of Rockingham, North Carolina, and grandfather of Rev. R. H. W. Leak, a prominent minister in the A. M. E. Conference of North Carolina, is said to have been hanged in Rockingham, North Carolina, charged with indorsing the Nat Turner Insurrection, because in a private conversation with his family he related to them something of what Nat Turner was doing in Southampton, where he had lately been on a visit to his grandmother. According to the account of Mr. W. H. Quick, he was taken by a mob at a camp-meeting, and tried and hung in the same month, in the year 1831.

Madison Washington was the name of a brave slave who, being a part of a cargo of 135 slaves en route to New Orleans from Virginia, when the boat was eight days out organized the slaves, made an onslaught on the officers, took possession of the boat and carried it to Nassau, an English possession, where England gave them protection, refusing to surrender them as "murderers and mutineers to perish on Southern gibbets."

---

* One author says: Upwards of one hundred slaves were slaughtered in the Southampton Tragedy, many of them in cold blood while walking in the streets—and about sixty white persons. Some of the alleged conspirators had their noses and ears cut off, the flesh of their cheeks cut out, their jaws broken asunder, and in that condition they were set up as marks to be shot at.

The Kindness of Washington in dressing the Captain's wounds and protecting and caring for his wife and children, marked him as a most magnanimous foe. Only one white man of the twelve commanding the ship was killed. He having fired into the slaves came at them with a spike; thereupon he was stabbed by one of Washington's men, who wrenched a bowie-knife from the hands of the Captain. Washington's only wish was, not blood, but freedom, which he gained.

"THE VIRGINIA MAROONS.

The Famous Dismal Swamp, some fifty miles long, extending from Norfolk, Virginia, into North Carolina, was a noted rendezvous for runaway slaves before the civil war. It is estimated that the slave property in this swamp was worth a million and a half dollars. They carried on a secret trade with the Virginia merchants, but any merchant caught fostering these people by trading with them was punished severely by law. The traders who were pursued found shelter among the maroons of the swamp. The chivalry of the Old Dominion never dared venture into this colony, and blood-hounds sent in came out no more. The Dismal Swamp colony continued from generation to generation, defying and outwitting the slave-owners right in the midst of one of the strongest slave-holding communities in the South.

"THE AMISTAD CAPTIVES."

Fifty-four Africans on board the Spanish slave-schooner "Amistad," under Captain Ramon Ferrer, on June 28, 1839, sailed from Havana, Cuba, for Porto Principe, another place on the island of Cuba, about three hundred miles distant from Havana. The fifty-four slaves were just from Lemboko, their native country in Africa. Joseph Cinquez, son of an African prince, was among them. He was shrewd, brave and intelligent. He looked on with disgust at the cruel treatment given him and his fellow-slaves, some being "chained down between the decks—space not more than four feet—by their wrists and ankles; forced to eat rice, sick or well, and whipped upon the slightest provocation." Cinquez witnessed the brutality· as long as his noble nature would allow, and when they were about five nights out from Havana, he chose a company of confederates from among his brethren and made an assault on the captain of the boat, and took him and his crew prisoners. Two sailors struck out for land when they found their captain and cook in chains, and left the boat in full possession of the Negroes. The man at the helm (Montes) was ordered to steer direct for Africa, under pain of death. This he did by day, but at night would make towards the coast of America. Finally, after continual wandering, the vessel was cited off the coast of the United States in August. All the ports were notified, and a number of revenue cutters were dispatched after her. She was finally captured on the 26th of August, 1839, by Lieut. Gidney of the United States Navy, and the "Amistad" and her fifty-four Africans were landed in New London, Connecticut. The two Spaniards found on board the vessel were examined by the United States officials, and the whole number of Africans were bound over to await trial as pirates. They being unable to give bond of course went to prison, but not to stay long. Public sentiment was everywhere aroused in their favor. The anti-slavery friends organized schools among them; the Africans learned rapidly and soon told all the details of the capture of the "Amistad" in English from their own lips without an interpreter. The trial occupied several months, during which they busied themselves in cultivating a garden of fifteen acres in a most skillful and intelligent manner. Their grievances were told all over America, and aroused the sympathies of the people. Finally, the court decided that the "Amistad captives" were not slaves but freemen. A thrill of joy passed through many an American heart, as well as their own, and when the news of this decision spread abroad, subscriptions began to come in. Mr. Lewis Tappan took a lively interest in the Africans, and in one way and another soon got together enough money to send them home to Africa, where they so much wanted to go. "If 'Merica men offered me as much gold as fill this cap," said one, "and give me houses, land and everything, so dat I stay in this country, I say No! No!! I want to see my father, my mother, my brother, my sister." One said, "We owe everything to God; He keeps us alive, and makes us free. When we go home to Mendi, we tell our brethren about God, Jesus Christ and Heaven." One was asked, if he was again captured and about to be sold into slavery, would he murder the captain and cook of another vessel, and if he wouldn't pray for rather than kill them? Cinquez heard it and replied, shaking his head, "Yes; I would pray for 'em and kill 'em, too."

These people were sent to Sierra Leone in Africa in company with five sainted missionaries. Great Britain sent them from Sierra Leone to their homes, and thus their efforts for freedom were successful.

CHAPTER XVIII.

ANTI-SLAVERY AGITATION.

Slavery or No Slavery was the question now before the American people. Millions of tracts, pamphlets, circulars and newspapers, besides the ministers and orators of the North, were now making sentiment against slavery. The people of the North were aroused.

The Census of 1850 gave a population of three and one-half million slaves in America, and they lived in the States of Delaware, New Jersey, Maryland, Virginia, North Carolina, South Carolina, Georgia, Florida, Alabama, Mississippi, Louisiana, Texas, Arkansas, Utah Territory, Kentucky, Missouri and Tennessee. Soon after this New Jersey, Delaware and Maryland freed their slaves.

The Political Parties were forced to take up the slavery question. The politicians were wily, and yielded to both sides for policy's sake. The South opposed every legislative act that favored the abolition of slavery. The great Daniel Webster hesitated to take a decided stand either way, and in 1858 Charles Sumner, a staunch anti-slavery man, came to the Senate from Massachusetts in Webster's place. Mr. Sumner said more and did more for the freedom of the slave than any of the great statesmen of his time. He offered no compromise, and asked only for *liberty* to the slaves.

The Fugitive Slave Law* allowed masters to capture their slaves in any State of the Union. Hence arose the underground railroad, which was a secret system for transporting runaway slaves into Canada. Some slaves were sent in boxes, and some carried in the night from one person to another until they reached the Canadian line. A great many runaway slaves made good their escape through this system.†

New States coming into the Union caused great discussion as to whether they should come in as free States or slave States. *Civil war* broke out in Kansas between the inhabitants of that Territory who wanted, and those who did not want, slaves. The anti-slavery people were led by John Brown, afterwards the leader in an attempt to capture the arsenal at Harper's Ferry, Virginia, and arm the slaves. He was hung as an insurrectionist.

Opposition in the North to the Abolitionists

---

* It was Chief Justice Taney who, in giving his decision on this law in the Dred-Scott case, said: "A Negro has no rights which a white man is bound to respect."

† See *Underground Railroad*, by William Still.

was manifested by the commercial people, who saw nothing in the whole question but the dollars and cents which they hoped to make out of the slave's products of cotton, tobacco, sugar, and rice. But the agitation continued.

Abraham Lincoln, endorsed by the anti-slavery people, was proposed as the Republican candidate for President in 1860, whereupon South Carolina declared if Lincoln was elected she would secede from the Union. Lincoln was elected, and accordingly South Carolina seceded, and was soon followed by the other slave-holding States.

CHAPTER XIX.

EXAMPLES OF UNDERGROUND RAILROAD WORK.

WILLIAM and Ellen Craft were slaves in the State of Georgia. Their hearts yearned for freedom. Their minds were at once set to work to formulate some plan of escape. It was at last settled. Ellen being very fair, while William was dark, was to pass for a young invalid planter, William being her slave and servant. Not being able to write, and without beard, she put her hand into a sling and tied her face up; after putting on male attire they were ready to start out. William attended to all the business, such as registering at the hotels and buying tickets. They stopped at a first-class hotel in Charleston, and also in Richmond, finally reaching Philadelphia safely. Ellen gave up her male attire, untied her face, released her arm from the sling, and her speech came to her. They put themselves under the care of the Abolitionists, were sent to Boston, but after the passage of the Fugitive Slave Bill, attempts were made to capture and put them back into slavery again. They were at last sent to England, where they remained for nearly twenty years; then they returned and made their home in Savannah, Georgia, where, we learn, they are still living.

CHAPTER XX.

THE SLAVE POPULATION OF 1860.

In the sixteen slave States there were 3,950,000 slaves in 1860, and 251,000 free colored people. Nearly 3,000,000 of the slaves were in the rural districts of the South; and the slave products of cotton, tobacco, rice, sugar-cane, hemp, and molasses, amounted to about $136,505,435. These products, made by slave labor, formed the basis of Southern prosperity. The war of the rebellion which commenced in the following year, was destined to shake the very foundation of Southern civilization. From a people unaccustomed to hard work, it was to take away those who worked for them, and those same people who were to be taken away were to be regaled in the priceless boon of citizenship. Let us now study some of the efforts of Negroes in helping to achieve this citizenship, after which we shall see how well they deserved to be citizens.

CHAPTER XXI.

THE WAR OF THE REBELLION.

ENLISTMENT OF NEGROES.

The Secession of South Carolina and the other Southern States was the signal for war. True to its declaration to do so, this State seceded when Lincoln was inaugurated in 1861. *Fort Sumter* was fired on by the Confederates and captured. The North was divided on the question of slavery, and the Government at Washington was slow in making any efforts to stop the rebellion. A few troops were sent into the field with the hope of frightening the South.

The *Battle of Bull Run* was fought, and disgracefully lost to the Union. It took some losses and failures to make the North believe the South would fight. Finally, after the defeat at Bull Run,

Lincoln issued a Proclamation for 75,000 volunteers. But the motto was, *no blacks need apply*. There was great prejudice in the North against he Negro's enlisting to fight for his freedom, and the President was also opposed to it.

The Confederates were already forming Negro companies for the defence of Richmond and building fortifications. The third and fourth regiments of Georgia showed one Negro company as they passed through Augusta en route to Virginia. Free Negroes enlisted on the Confederate side at New Orleans and Memphis. They were highly spoken of by the Southern papers. But the North seemed to think still that to put the Negro in the Union blue would disgrace that uniform.

General Hunter, stationed at Port Royal, South Carolina, did not agree with Congress nor the President. When he succeeded General Sherman, instructions from the Secretary of War to "accept the services of all *loyal* persons" were handed him; and he seized this opportunity (there being nothing said about Negroes) to enlist a Negro regiment of fugitive slaves. His conduct was inquired into by Mr. Wickliffe, a Congressman from Kentucky, and a resolution of censure was offered.

Major-General Hunter replied to the inquiry made in Congress as to his enlisting slaves, that the Negroes seemed to be the only loyal people in that locality, and they were anxious to fight for their freedom, and gave every evidence of making "invaluable auxiliaries." They knew the country and were accustomed to the climate.

General Phelps, stationed in Louisiana about this time, was making a bold fight for the enlistment of Negroes in and around New Orleans. He was opposed by General Benj. F. Butler, who protested so strongly against it that finally General Phelps was forced to resign and return to his home in Vermont. The sentiment of the Northern army seemed to have a conspicuous leaning towards admitting the right of the South to hold slaves. General Butler refused the runaway slayes quarters in his headquarters. McClellan, a reeking failure as a commander, said, with others, that if he thought he was fighting to free the "niggers" he would sheath his sword. He soon failed in the Virginia campaign and was forced to resign.

Mr. Stevens proposed a bill in Congress authorizing the President to "raise and equip 150,000 soldiers of African descent" Meanwhile Col. Thomas W. Higginson and Col. Montgomery, with a company of Negro troops were ascending the St. John River, in Florida, where he captured Jacksonville, which had been abandoned by white Union Troops. Among those who favored Mr. Stevens' measure were Horace Greeley and Edwin M. Stanton, who seemed to have been convinced of the worth of the colored troops from the testimony of such men as Phelps, Higginson, Hunter, and Montgomery, who had already seen what Negro troops could accomplish.

Public Sentiment was being aroused on the subject. The newspapers discussed the matter. The

New York *Tribune* said: "Drunkenness, the bane of our army, does not exist among the black troops." "Nor have I yet discovered the slightest ground of inferiority to white troops." *Mr. Lincoln* very soon changed his mind, Congress gave its consent, and the order went forth to enlist Negroes in defence of the Union.

The Right to Fight for what they thought would ultimately end in their freedom was hailed with shouts of joy wherever the tidings reached the Negroes.

At Newbern, N. C., they made a great demonstration. The enlisting places at New Orleans and other Southern cities then in the hands of the Federals were the scenes of the wildest confusion in the mad rush of the colored people to register their names on the army records.

A Difficulty arose in getting sufficient arms for all the colored troops; and a further difficulty was to be met in selecting white officers who had the courage to brave public sentiment and take the command of Negro troops. Negro daring and excellency on the battle-field soon broke down these flimsy weaknesses of the white officers, and the summer of 1863 found over 100,000 Negroes in the Union ranks, and over 50,000 armed and equipped on the fields of battle.

Their Pay was seven dollars per month, with

board and clothing. The whites received thirteen dollars per month with board and clothing. Thus the former slave went forth to meet his master on the battle-field, sometimes to capture or be captured ; sometimes to fall side by side, one pierced with the Southern, the other with the Northern bayonet.

EMANCIPATION PROCLAMATIONS.

Two Proclamations were issued by Mr. Lincoln. The first, on the 22d of September, 1862, defined the issue of the war to be " for the object of practically restoring the constitutional relation between the United States and each of the States, and the people thereof." It offered, first, to pay the masters for their slaves and colonize them in America or Africa. Second, it proposed to free the slaves of those persons and States then engaged in actual rebellion. Third, it offered to pay from the Federal treasury loyal masters who had lost their slaves in and during the rebellion.

The Second Proclamation was issued January 1, 1863, and is the one we celebrate. This measure was urged upon Mr. Lincoln by the Abolitionists and those who wished the Negro free. It did not free all the slaves. Some counties were left out. Though the Abolitionists saw in the proclamation the consummation of their prayers and hopes, Mr.

Lincoln and his Cabinet evidently regarded the proclamation as a war measure, very necessary under the circumstances, to shorten the war. The South would have surrendered in half the time had not a large number of slaves remained on the plantations raising supplies for the Confederate army, and supporting and protecting their masters' families.

CHAPTER XXII.

EMPLOYMENT OF NEGRO SOLDIERS.

Mr. Williams Says: "All history, ancient and modern, Pagan and Christian, justified the conduct of the Federal Government in the employment of slaves as soldiers. Greece had tried the experiment, and at the battle of Marathon there were two regiments composed of slaves. The beleagured city of Rome offered freedom to her slaves who would volunteer as soldiers, and at the battle of Cannæ a regiment of Roman slaves made Hannibal's cohorts reel before their unequalled courage. Negro officers, as well as soldiers, had shared the perils and glories of the campaigns of Napoleon Bonaparte; and even the Royal Guard at the Court of Imperial France had been mounted with black soldiers. In two wars in North America, Negro soldiers had followed the fortunes of military life and won the applause of white patriots on two continents. So, then, all history furnished a precedent for the guidance of the United States Government in the civil war of America."

Just How Well the Negro Soldiers Behaved may be gathered from a description of

SOME FAMOUS BATTLES IN WHICH NEGROES FOUGHT.

Port Hudson, May 27, 1863. The Negro regiment under Col. Nelson was assigned the difficult task of taking this fort, which seemed almost impregnable. It was situated on a high bluff overlooking the river in front. Around the sides and rear, close under the bluff, ran a bayou twelve feet deep and from fifteen to twenty feet wide. Looking out from openings in the embankment were the grim mouths of many deadly cannon. They were arranged so as to make a straight raking charge on the front of any approaching force, while a score and a half of heavy guns were to cut down the left and right wings with grape and canister.

Having marched All Night, the "Black Regiment" stacked arms at 5 A.M. One hour was given for rest and breakfast. Many, completely overcome by the enervating heat and dust, sank down "in their tracks" and slept.

The Officers received their instructions at 5.30, and at 6 o'clock the bugle sounded. "Fall in !" was heard ringing out among the soldiers ; and the scene reminded one more of a holiday party than a march to death. The troops seemed anxious to fight. The white troops looked on with uneasiness and doubts concerning the Negro's courage. The Confederates in the fort ridiculed the idea that Negroes were to charge them,

The Negro Regiment moved towards the fort. There was death-like silence, save the tramp of soldiers and the tap of drum. "Forward; double-quick, march!" rang out along the line; not a piece was fired. Now the Confederate guns open on the left; one shell kills twelve men. "Right *about!*" was the command; the regiment wheeled to the right for about three hundred yards, then coolly and steadily faced the enemy again by companies.

Six Deathly charges were thus made, when Col. Nelson reported to Gen. Dwight his inability to take the fort because of the bayou being too deep for the men to wade. Gen. Dwight replied: "I shall consider that he has accomplished nothing unless he takes those guns." The soldiers saw it was impossible, as well as Col. Nelson, yet "*again the order to charge*" was obeyed with a shout.

Captain Andre Callioux commanded Company E in the next charge. He marched his colored brethren over the dead bodies of their comrades, crying, "Follow me!" and while flashing his sword within fifty yards of the belching Confederate guns, he was smitten down in front of his company by a shell.

Color-Sergeant Anselmas Planciancois said to Col. Nelson, before the fight: "Colonel, I will bring back these colors to you in honor, or report to God the reason why." It was now between 11 and 12

o'clock in the morning.   The fight began at 7 A.M.
The gallant Callioux was lying dead on the field.
His men now charged almost in the mouth of the
Confederate guns.   Planciancois bore the flag in
front.   A shell strikes the staff and blows off half
of the brave sergeant's head; he falls, wrapped in
the folds of his nation's flag, his brains scattered
amid them, but still his strong grip holds the staff
even in death, till

Corporal Heath catches it up to bear it to the
front again.   Pierced by a musket-ball which split
his head, he, too, falls upon the body of the brave
Planciancois.   Still another corporal lifts the flag
and bears it through the fray.   And thus the Negro
troops, on almost their very first trial, silenced all
clamors as to their bravery.   Port Hudson was not
taken then, but the reason for defeat lay not in a
lack of unrivalled daring and heroic courage on the
part of the Negro troops.   The loss was 37 killed
and wounded, and missing 271.

The New York Times says of this battle: " Gen.
Dwight, at least, must have had the idea not only that
they (Negro troops) were men, but something more
than men from the terrific test to which he put their
valor.   The deeds of heroism performed by these
men were such as the proudest white men might
emulate.   Their colors are literally bespattered with
blood and brains.

"The color-sergeant of the 1st Louisiana, on being mortally wounded, hugged the colors to his breast, when a struggle ensued between the two color corporals on each side of him as to who should have the honor of bearing the sacred standard. One black lieutenant actually mounted the enemy's works four times. . . . . Although repulsed in an attempt which —situated as things were—was all but impossible, these regiments, though badly cut up, were still on hand, and burning with a passion ten times hotter from their fierce baptism of blood."

General Banks wrote, concerning the " Black Regiment" at Port Hudson : "It gives me pleasure to report that they answered every expectation. Their conduct was heroic." The success of the Negro troops at Port Hudson rang in the halls of Congress, in the lecture-room, in the pulpit, in the newspapers ; poets sang of it, and Northern orators vied with each other in eloquent pictures of the scene of that great fight which settled the question as to the Negro's fitness for the army.

Milliken's Bend, 6th of June, 1863. The Confederates came up from Louisiana, about 3000 strong. They rested over night, while the Federals were collecting at the temporary fort in the bend of the Mississippi. The Union men of war " Choctaw " and "Lexington·" appeared, coming up the river before daylight, on the morning of the 6th of June, which·

was the time the Confederates made their first charge, yelling, "No quarter to Negroes and their officers!" The Negro troops were without training, being lately recruited, but they fought like veterans. The Confederates fell back under their heavy fire in front, and charged the Union flanks. Upon this the Union troops found shelter from the gun-boats, and broadside after broadside made the Confederates hasten away.

An Eye Witness' Description: "As before stated, the Confederates drove our force towards the gun-boats, taking colored men prisoners. This so enraged them that they rallied and charged the enemy more heroically and desperately than has been recorded during the war. It was a genuine bayonet charge, a hand-to-hand fight, that has never occurred to any extent during this prolonged conflict. Upon both sides men were killed with the butts of muskets. White and colored men were lying side by side pierced by bayonets, and in some instances transfixed to the earth. One brave man took his former master prisoner, and brought him into camp with great gusto. A Confederate prisoner made a particular request that *his own* Negroes should not be placed over him as a guard.

"Union loss one hundred killed, five hundred wounded, mostly Negroes. Confederate loss two hundred killed, five hundred wounded, two hundred taken prisoners, and two cannon."

The battles of Fort Pillow and Milliken's Bend made many friends for the colored soldiers. Their soldierly qualities were on trial; the experiment of arming Negroes to fight for the Union was being tried. This the colored troops seemed to realize, and it stimulated them to do their very best. They fought courageously, and fully satisfied all doubts concerning their valor.

The Draft Riot broke out in New York in July, 1863. An order came from Washington, authorizing soldiers to be drafted in New York City. The Democratic newspapers ridiculed the idea of the people's being drafted into service "to fight the battles of 'niggers and Abolitionists.'" General Wood finally put down the riot after killing thirteen of the rioters, wounding eighteen and taking twenty-four prisoners. "They had burned the Colored Orphan's Asylum, hung colored men to lamp-posts, and destroyed the property of this class of citizens with impunity."

The 54th Massachusetts was the first colored regiment organized in the free States, Colonel Shaw commander. It played a prominent part in the attempt to take *Fort Wagner*, near Charleston, S. C. It marched two days and nights through swamps and drenching rains to be in time for the assault. Soaking wet, muddy, hungry and fatigued,

Fort Wagner.

they reached the field in time and gladly accepted the "post of honor and danger," immediately in front. After a five minutes' rest they double-quicked a half-mile to the fort, where, after a most gallant and desperate fight, *Sergeant William H. Carney* planted the regimental flag on the works. Nearly all the officers of the regiment were killed, and it was led off by a boy—Lieut. Higginson.

"**Sergeant Carney,**" says an eye witness, "received a severe wound in the thigh, but fell only upon his knees. He planted the flag upon the parapet, lay on the outer slope, that he might get as much shelter as possible ; there he remained for over half an hour, till the second brigade came up. He kept his colors flying till the second conflict was ended. When our forces retired, he followed, creeping on one knee, still holding the flag." When he entered the hospital (bleeding from one wound in the head and another in the thigh) "his wounded comrades cheered him," and he said, "*Boys, the old flag never touched the ground.*"

The Negro Soldiers. The sentiment against the Negro at the North had somewhat abated in the face of the irresistible bravery as exhibited by Negro troops at Wagner and Port Hudson. The North saw that wonderful results could be achieved by Negro soldiers.

The Confederates exchanged before this some Union officers, but refused to exchange Negroes.

CHAPTER XXIII.

FORT PILLOW.

THIS fort is located on the east bank of the Mississippi, about fifty miles above Memphis, in Tennessee.   It crowned the top of a steep bluff, covered with trees and shrubbery.   Major L. F. Booth was in command with a garrison of 557 men, 262 of whom were colored.   There were six artillery pieces.   Gen. N. B. Forest, commanding a large force of Confederate cavalry, appeared at the fort at sunrise on the 13th of April, 1864, and demanded its surrender.   Major Booth drew up his force in the intrenchments around the parapet.   Thus a continual firing was kept up till the afternoon, during which Major Booth was killed.   Major Bradford took command.   The firing ceased for the guns to cool off and to be cleaned.   Meanwhile, under a flag of truce, Gen. Forest demanded the surrender of the fort, stating, " If I have to storm your works, you may expect no quarter."   The Confederates, taking advantage of the truce, were hiding in the trenches from which Major Bradford had withdrawn his men into the fort.   A few moments later they rushed in with their deafening yell—"No quarter!"

The Union troops offered stubborn resistance, but, with superior numbers crowding in from front, rear, and sides, they were overcome and surrendered.

The War in the West was now about at an end. Sherman set out upon his famous march through Georgia ; Grant, having opened up the Mississippi, marched on Richmond, which had now become the strategic point of the war. McClellan, Hooker, Meade, and Burnside, had failed in their assaults on this the Confederate capital. All hopes were now centred on Grant. To him was assigned the task, and this brings us to the

CAMPAIGN IN VIRGINIA, 1864.

Twenty Thousand Strong marched the Negro troops into the campaign of Virginia. On their way they passed through Washington. Mr. Lincoln, with General Burnsides and friends, reviewed the long line from the balcony of Willard's Hotel. As the long, heavy columns filed past, the President acknowledged their almost continuous "Hurrah for Lincoln!" He was deeply touched by the spectacle ; there were tears in many eyes that saw the brave thousands of sable sons, but a little while ago slaves.

now gallantly marching to defend the Union. It was a scene never forgotten by those who saw it.

With Equal Pay, a recognition as soldiers by Mr. Davis, and a brilliant record, marched the Negro troops into the Virginia campaign. Gen. Butler, who was now convinced by the scenes at Port Hudson, Forts Pillow and Wagner, of the Negro's capacity for fighting, was stationed at Bermuda Hundreds with a large corps of Negro troops.

Grant threw his Forces across the Rapidan and met the Confederates in *The Wilderness.* He left Gen. Ferrero with his colored troops to protect his wagon train in the rear. *Ewell* with the Confederate cavalry whipped around in search of these supplies. Gen. Ferrero with his Negro troops met Ewell. The Confederates made a bold charge and captured twenty-seven wagons. The hungry soldiers prepared to feast on their plunder.

Gen. Ferrero opened fire. The Confederates charged again, giving the colored troops their very best, but the Negro regiments did not budge. Gen Ferrero then ordered his troops to charge, and, in this the first fight between Negro troops and Virginians, the Confederates were driven "as the gale drives chaff." " It was the first time at the East," says Gen. Badeau, in his Military History of Grant, " when the colored troops had been engaged in any important battle, and the display of soldierly qualities won a frank acknowledgment from both troops and commanders, not all of whom had before been willing to look upon Negroes as comrades. But after that time, white soldiers in the Army of the Potomac were not displeased to receive the support of the black ones; they had found the support worth having."

CHAPTER XXIV.

AROUND PETERSBURG.

HERE it was that Negro soldiers covered themselves with merited glory in the presence of white troops on both sides; surprising in their daring to officers trained at West Point, and that, too, on the very soil where slavery first made its appearance in this country.

The City of Petersburg lies on the Appomattox river near the James, and not far from Richmond, with which it has railroad connection, and formed the base of supplies up the James for the troops in defence of Richmond. It therefore became an important point to reduce. It was strongly fortified on all sides for miles out.

The Task of Taking the " Cockade City," as it was called, fell to Gen. Smith, assisted by Gen. Kautz, coming up on the east, Brooks following Kautz; Martindale, who was to move up the Appomattox, and Hinks, who moved between the two. *The Black Brigade* was under Gen. Hinks, who discovered a Confederate battery on a knoll six miles out from the city. Under range of the Confederate guns he formed his line for a charge. The battery must be taken at the point of the bayonet. "Forward!" rang out along the line, and as the troops cleared the woods, the enemy opened a raking fire with canister, siege-gun and musket. But away swept the black brigade, their ranks shattered with deadly shells. As they closer came, a fusilade of musketry came down upon them; a hundred men fell; but leaping and dashing, with a wild cheer, they burst over the bulwarks, drove the enemy from their guns, and instantly turned them on their scattered ranks beating a hasty retreat towards Petersburg—and the colored troops had won the day.

Brooks and Martindale were now in front of the Confederates' main line near the river. Hinks, with his Negro corps of 3000, was ordered towards "Dunn's House," three miles from the city on the road leading east.

To Reach His Position it was necessary to cross an open space in full reach of the sharp-shooters and artillery of the enemy. They crossed this space by moving forward a few paces and then lying down; at every quiet moment they would steal forward; they thus reached their position under the most trying test. But on reaching their post, so thick and deadly was the firing from all sides that they dared not rise; so thus they lay from one till five o'clock P.M., while torrents of lead whizzed over their heads.

"**Dunn's House**" was defended by three forts, one in front, one north, and another south. Deep ravines lay in front, while an almost impassable abatis of trees impeded the way to the forts. Seven hundred yards in front lay Hinks' black troops hungry for the fray. Thus they lay in deep suspense, anxious for orders to go forward. Meanwhile, shells plowed the earth around them for four long hours, which seemed to them like days.

At Five o'clock the command "Forward!" was greeted with a rush and a shout. The brave Negro troops went forward at a double-quick; the skirmishers were the first to reach the embankments, and were greeted with a shower of bullets which tumbled many headlong and lifeless into the pits. But on came the main body as if impelled by lightning; they swept into the midst of the enemy, grabbed their guns and fired them upon them as they "ran for their lives." Three hundred Confederates were taken prisoners, and several pieces of artillery were captured.

Smith Had Petersburg now at his mercy. Brooks and Martindale had swept the enemy in front of them simultaneously with Hinks, and the way was open to march immediately into the city. Gen. Smith, however, decided to wait for the arrival of Gen. Birney with the Second Corps—and this delay caused the loss of many thousand lives.

Next Morning, as the·sun.peeped up over the yellow waters of the Appomattox, the condition of things had changed. The flower of Lee's army had come up in the night-time, and Grant was compelled afterwards to lay siege to the city, under which it finally surrendered.

Secretary Stanton was wild with delight over the valor of the colored troops at Petersburg. Said he : " The hardest fighting was done by the black troops. The forts they stormed were the worst of all. After the affair was over, Gen. Smith went to thank them, and tell them he was proud of their courage and dash. He says they cannot be excelled as soldiers, and that hereafter he will send them in a difficult place as readily as the white troops."

CHAPTER XXV.

THE CRATER.

Petersburg was now surrounded by the Union army. There was continual skirmishing. Burnside commanded the Ninth Corps, composed partly of Negro troops. By fierce fighting he made his way up to within a hundred and fifty yards of the Confederate batteries. Projecting out in front of them was a strong fort. After consultation a trench was dug out some hundred and fifty yards long, branching off in two directions at the end under the fort. It was packed with powder and explosives, the design being to blow the place up. As arranged, on the 30th of July, 1864, the match was applied. Dampness prevented an explosion. Lieut. Jacob Douty and Sergeant Henry Rus volunteered to go into the trenches and ascertain and remove the difficulty, and very soon after they came out, at 4.45 A.M., the match was again applied, and—read the result, by Gen. Badeau: " The mine explòded with a shock like that of an earthquake, tearing up the Confederates' works above them, and vomiting men, guns and caissons, two hundred feet into the air. The tremendous mass appeared for a moment to hang suspended in the heavens like a huge indented cone, the exploding powder still flashing out here and there, while limbs and bodies of mutilated men, and fragments of cannon and wood-work, could be seen. Then all fell heavily to the ground again, with a second report like thunder. When the smoke and dust had cleared away, only an enormous crater, thirty feet deep, sixty feet wide, and a hundred and fifty feet long, stretched out in front of the Ninth Corps, where the Confederate fort had been."

At the moment of the explosion the Union batteries belched forth from one hundred and ten deadly cannon and fifty mortars, and verily the earth seemed to tremble from the shock.

The Plan was to follow the discharge of the batteries with a charge. Gen. Burnside had arranged his Negro troops for the post of honor. A dispute arose between him and Gen. Meade as to the wisdom of this plan. The whole matter was referred to Gen. Grant, who ordered *lots to be drawn* by the different Generals as to " who should go into the crater." The lot fell on Gen. Ledlie. Gen. Ledlie accordingly endeavored to draw up his troops into the mouth of the crater. The Tenth New Hampshire faltered and broke ranks. Generals Potter and Wilcox marched their troops into the dreadful hole, where they halted long enough for the Confederates to make an attack.

Gen. Potter Struggled out with his division and charged the enemy, but had to retire. Gen. Burnside now ordered his colored troops around the edges of the crater; the Confederates were now gathering around from all sides, and under a heavy fire drove the colored troops into the deadly hole, from which they continued to rally until nightfall.

A Ridiculous Mistake was made by the Federals in not marching into the city immediately after the explosion, when the Confederates were nonplussed and breaking away in mad confusion. *Gen. Grant* says of this disgraceful affair: "The four divisions of his (Burnside's) corps were commanded by Generals Potter, Wilcox, Ledlie and Ferrero. The last was a colored division; and Burnside selected it to make the assault. Meade interfered with this. Burnside then took Ledlie's division."

Before the committee that investigated the affair Gen. Grant said: "General Burnside wanted to put his colored division in front, I believe if he had done so it would have been a success."

Four Thousand Four Hundred Union soldiers perished through the mistake then of not allowing the colored troops to take the Confederate works which Gen. Grant says they would have taken.

How the Colored Soldiers fought in the *crater*, let the Confederate commanders (some of whose slaves were there) speak: "Ah, boys, you have got hot work ahead—they are Negroes and show no quarter." (Col. Stewart.)

"**Encouraged, Threatened, Emulating** the white troops, the black men fought with desperation. *Some Confederate soldiers recognized their slaves* at the crater. A Captain of the Forty-first Virginia gave the military salute to 'Bob' and 'Ben,' whom he had left hoeing corn in Dinwiddie."

Petersburg being Captured, the siege of Richmond was begun with a vigor and determination such as only a Grant could command. Meanwhile, a lively discussion was going on at the Confederate capital as to the proposition of Mr. Benjamin to arm the slaves in defence of the city. Gen. Lee and Mr. Jefferson Davis favored this plan, and recommended that such colored people as would join the Confederate ranks should be set free.

Some Score or More Blacks, three of whom were Mr. Benjamin's slaves, enlisted and were daily drilled in the capitol square, which stands on an eminence in the centre of the city.

Gen. Lee was now employing his best troops and military manœuvres to keep Grant out of the Confederate capital. His retreats and skirmishes, executed with genius and tact, delayed the event; but opposed by superior numbers, his army half-starved, and the Confederacy subjugated in the Southwest, he saw the uselessness of a further hopeless sacrifice of his men, and *surrendered accordingly* at Appomattox, on the 9th of April, 1865, " he, and his army, defeated in every way possible, numbering 27,516," and " every man was fed by the conqueror."

When the Union Army marched into Richmond, the Confederates set the city on fire, and commenced a wholesale destruction and plunder of everything. Thousands of gallons of rum were emptied into the streets, and staggering destruction of everything useful seemed in order. The colored troops were · organized into fire brigades, and soon extinguished the fires and stopped the plunder their masters had begun.

CHAPTER XXVI.

INCIDENTS OF THE WAR.

Rodman's Point, N. C., was the scene of a brave deed by a Negro. A flat-boat full of troops, with a few colored soldiers among them, tried to land at this place. The Confederate soldiers were lying in wait for the boat, and the soldiers in it could only save themselves by lying flat on the bottom out of reach of their deadly guns. But if the boat remained where it was very long it would be surrounded and captured. One of the colored soldiers saw the danger, and knowing the boat must be pushed off or all would be killed, suddenly rose up and said: "Somebody got to die to get us all out dis 'ere, and it mout jes as well be me as anybody!" Saying this he deliberately stepped on shore and pushed the boat off. The men in the bottom were saved, but the Negro hero's body "fell forward into the end of the boat pierced by five bullets." He had done what no other of them dared do to save the lives of his comrades.

A Negro Established a Clothes-line Tele-graph in the Falmouth camp on the Rappahannock in 1863. The Confederate and Union armies occupied opposite sides of the river and used every means of gaining knowledge of each other's movements. The colored attendant in the Union camp proved very valuable here as elsewhere during the war. A colored man named Dabney drifted into the Union lines one day from a neighboring farm, and soon proved very useful because of his full knowledge of the topography of the country. He was given employment as "cook and body servant." He became much interested in the system of army signals employed, and begged to have them explained to him. This was done, and he learned them readily. His wife soon came over, and after staying awhile was allowed to return as servant to a "secesh woman" whom General Hooker was about to send to her friends on the other side. She went over and took a place as laundress at "the headquarters of a prominent rebel General." Dabney, her husband, was on the Union side, and soon began to know all about what was to take place in the Confederate camp. An hour or two before any movement took place he could tell all about it, and it always turned out as he said. The wonder and puzzle to the Union men was how he got his information, as he didn't seem to neglect his work to go off for any information, and did not converse with the scouts. After numerous questions and many requests he finally took one of the officers to a prominent point near by, and pointed out a cabin on the banks of the river in the suburbs of the enemy's camp. He asked the officer if he saw a clothes-line with clothes hanging on it. The officer replied "Yes," whereupon Dabney said : "Well, that clothes-line tells me in half an hour just what goes on in their camp. You see, my wife over there, she washes for the officers, and cooks and waits around, and as soon as she hears of any movement or anything going on she comes down and moves the clothes on that line so I can understand it in a minute. That there gray shirt is Longstreet, and when she takes it off it means he's gone down about Richmond. That white shirt means Hhl, and when she moves it up to the west end of the line, Hill's Corps has moved up stream. That red one is Stonewall. He's down on the right now, and if he moves she will move that red shirt." One morning Dabney came in and reported a movement over there, but said it "Don't mean anything, they are only making believe." An officer went out to look at the clothes-line telegraph through his field-glass. There had been quite a shifting over there of the army flannels. "But how do you know but there's something in it?" "Do you see those two blankets pinned together at the bottom?" said Dabney. "Yes, but what of it?" said the officer. "Why, that's her way of making a fish-trap ; and when she pins the clothes together that way, it means that Lee is only trying to draw us into his fish-trap." As long as the two armies lay watching each other on opposite banks of the stream, Dabney with his clothes-line telegraph continued to be one of the promptest and most reliable of General Hooker's scouts. (Taken from Civil War—Song and Story.)

William Staines, Hero of the Fight at Belmont, was servant to General McClernand. He was close by his employer during many an engagement. On one occasion, in the course of the fight, a captain of one of the companies was struck by a spent ball, which disabled him from walking. Staines, the colored servant, rode up to him and shouted, "Captain, if you can fight any longer for the Stars and Stripes, take my horse and lead your men." He then dismounted and helped the wounded officer into his saddle, and, as he was walking away, a rebel dragoon rushed forward at the officer to take him prisoner. The brave Staines did not flinch, but drew his revolver and put a ball through the rebel's head, scattering his brains over the horse's neck. (Revised from Civil War—Song and Story.)

CHAPTER XXVII.

THE END OF THE WAR.

For four years the American people had been fighting among themselves. At the outbreak of the struggle the freedom of the slaves was not looked for by many. But the Abolitionists, who grew stronger as the war progressed, pressed their views upon the leaders of the country. They took every advantage of every opportunity to make the freedom of the slaves the main issue of the war; and their efforts, coupled with the desire of the Union leaders to weaken the Confederacy by employing Negro troops, to whom they offered freedom, caused the final proclamation of Mr. Lincoln, in 1863, giving freedom to the slaves.

In this war there were employed on the Union side more than 186,000 colored soldiers, whose bravery stands vouched for by every Union, and many Confederate generals, who saw them as daring in the face of death as their fellow white soldiers.

On the Confederate Side, there were enlisted throughout the South, in various employments, some

6000 colored troops. But all over the South, while their masters were away at war, the Negro women and men were enlisted in the ranks of the private duties of the Southern soldiers' homes, which, ever be it remembered to the honor and credit of the Negro race of America, they protected faithfully and industriously. The opportunity for outrage and plunder was open on every side, but not a hurtful hand was laid on the thousands of white widows, orphans, and aged, who lay defenceless in the Negroes' power. This action on the part of the slaves proves that the race is not fond of bloodshed, and is kind even to its foes.

Some Plantations, on the contrary, were found in better trim on the return of the masters from the war than when they left them.

Negro Body-servants accompanied their masters into the war, shared the roughs of camp-life, and often were the last to minister to their wants in the hospital, and the first to bear the tidings home to the anxious family after death, taking with them sometimes the treasured watch or ring

Mr. James H. Jones,* of Raleigh, N C., served as messenger to Mr. Jefferson Davis during his

---

* He emphatically denies the assertion that has gained currency, to the effect that Mr. Jefferson Davis, while escaping from the Union forces was attired in female clothes. Mr. J. states that the Confederate President used a large cloak, which he usually wore indoors, to disguise himself with.

Presidency of the Confederacy at Richmond. He was with him when caught by the Union troops in southwest Georgia, and was also confined with him in the "Rip-Raps," at Hampton Roads, Virginia. After the war, Mr. Jones kept up a correspondence with Mr. Davis, until his death, and received a new photograph whenever Mr. Davis had a new one taken. Mr. Jones is now an honored citizen of Raleigh, and a member of the Board of Aldermen.

CHAPTER XXVIII.

RECONSTRUCTION, 1865-68.

After the Surrender of Lee at Appomattox, the question arose as to what should be done with the Southern States that for four years had rebelled against the flag of the Union, and had set up a flag of their own. The Southern flag was now conquered; and the plan of the North was to restore these conquered States into the Union. Amnesty was offered all those who desired it. A *Provisional Government* was first established in North Carolina, with W. W. Holden at its head; other States were organized in the same way. Conventions were called by the Provisional Governors of the several States, and new constitutions adopted in conformity with the Constitution of the United States.

The Right to Vote was denied the colored people. Exclusion from public places was established by law. *Thirty-nine* lashes was the punishment for keeping firearms. When white persons were implicated, colored people could not testify in the courts.

The Thirteenth Amendment to the Constitution, making the race citizens, was virtually made null and void by the legislatures of the reconstructed States. So it became necessary to pass *The Civil Rights Bill*, giving the colored people the right to enter public places, and ride on first-class railroad cars. This bill has been declared unconstitutional by our Supreme Court. Owing to the attempts of the Ku-Klux Klan to prevent colored people from voting, the fifteenth amendment was passed guaranteeing to them the right to vote and to have their votes counted. Thus, the eleven Southern States were reconstructed on a basis of universal suffrage, and the colored race began to develop statesmen, orators, lawyers, judges, teachers of various kinds, ministers, and discreet, far-seeing business men.

THE FREEDMEN'S BUREAU.

The design of this institution was to educate the newly emancipated colored people into all the ways of freedom. Schools were opened, to which there was a general rush, so great was the thirst for knowledge. Many gray heads could be seen among the children, and the "Blue Back Speller" was often to be seen even in the Sabbath-schools. Such a stampede, such an ardent desire for knowledge, was possibly never witnessed anywhere before. Many very old people learned to read the Bible, and the joy they seemed to get from this long coveted privilege was poured out in often thankful and fervent prayer.

Gen. O. O. Howard was a leading spirit in the establishment of the Freedmen's Bureau. His design was to make the colored people better citizens in every respect. With him was associated a saintly corps of devoted, missionary-inclined white men and women, who planted school-houses and churches in many a hamlet of this once slave-cursed but now free land.

Many of These People came from the best families of the North, were well educated, refined and cultured. Their pupils were not slow in catching the beautiful graces of these instructors, and their extra qualities are demonstrated in the wonderful educational progress the race has made within only twenty-six years of actual freedom.

The Plan was to locate schools at central points where teachers and preachers might be trained to go out into the rural districts in which the majority of the race still lived. The money was contributed by benevolent people of the North, and a wiser investment, both for God and humanity, was never made.

Through the Influence of the Freedmen's Bureau the Southern States got their present free-school system, which they did not have before the war. Some schools established during this time were: Shaw University, Raleigh, N. C.; Howard University, Washington, D. C.; Fisk University, Nashville, Tenn.; Atlanta University, Atlanta, Ga.; Hampton Normal School, Hampton, Va.; St. Augustine Normal School, Raleigh, and many others whose influence for good is incalculable.

CHAPTER XXIX.

PROGRESS SINCE FREEDOM.

Through a Century and a Half we have now traced our ancestors' history. We have seen how they performed the hard tasks assigned them by their masters: following the hoe and the plow with a laugh and a song; making magnificent estates, building mansions, furnishing them with the splendor of the times; so eager in patriotism as to be the first to shed their blood on the altar of their country's liberty. All this they did with no other hope of reward than a slave's cabin and a life of bondage for themselves and children. Scarcely have they ever sought revenge in riot or bloodshed. Stolen from a home of savage freedom they found themselves in strait circumstances as slaves in America, but the greatness of the Negro's nature crops out plainly in the wonderful way in which he adapted himself to his new conditions. The fact that he went to work willingly, worked so long and faithfully, and rebelled so little, marks him as far superior to the Indian, who never accepts the conditions of labor, either for himself or another; and univer-

sally enjoys the rank of a savage rather than that
of a civilized being. A plant placed in the window
of a dark chamber gradually bends its foliage towards
the sunlight; so the Negro, surrounded by the darkness of slavery, bent his life toward the light of his
master's God. He found Him. In Him he trusted,
to Him he prayed, from Him he hoped for deliverance; no people were ever more devout according
to their knowledge of the word, no people ever suffered persecution more bravely, no people ever got
more out of the few talents assigned them; and for
this humble devotion, this implicit trust and faith-
fulness, God has now rewarded them. The race
comes out of slavery with more than it had before it
went in. *But there was no need of any slavery at all.
Jamestown, New England,* and the other colonies
might have held the Negro long enough to serve
out his passage from Africa, and then given him his
freedom, as they did their white slaves imported
from England. The mistake was made then; the
mistake became a law which the people were educated to believe was just. Many *did not* believe it,
and some slaveholders sought to make the condition
of their slaves comfortable. The affection arising
between the slave and his master often governed
the treatment. The Negro being largely endowed
by nature with affection, affability, and a forgiving
spirit, generally won for himself good treatment.

Then, too, the master had some soul, and where that ingredient of his make-up was deficient, a selfish interest in the slave as his property somewhat modified the venom that might have more often visited itself upon the unfortunate slave in lashes and stripes.

Many Affections and Friendships formed between master and slave exist to the present day. Some slaves are still at the old homestead, conditions entirely reversed, voting differently at the polls, but *friends* at home ; and in death the family of one follows that of the other to the grave.

When the War Ended, the whole South was in an unsettled condition—property destroyed, thousands of her sons dead on the battle-field, no credit, conquered. But if the condition of the whites was bad, that of the blacks was *worse.* They were without homes, money, or learning. They were now to feed, clothe, and protect themselves in a goverment whose treasury they had enriched with two centuries and a half of unrequited labor, and a country whose laws they must obey but could not read.

It was Natural that they should make mistakes. But they made less mistakes than the *bummers* who came South for plunder during reconstruction times, and with the false promise of "forty acres and a mule," led the unlettered race into a season of idleness and vain hopes. But this condition did not last. The Negro inherited the ability to work from the institution of slavery. He soon set about to utilize this ability. I ask what race could have done more? And this the Negro has done, though virtually ostracized from the avenues of trade and speculation. His admission to a trades-union is the exception rather than the rule in America. A colored boy taking a place as porter in a store at the same time with a white boy, may find the white boy soon promoted to a clerkship, then to a partnership in the firm, if he is smart; but the colored boy remains, year after year, where he first commenced, no matter how worthy, no matter how competent. His lot is that of a menial; custom assigns him there, and in looking for clerks and partners he is not thought of by the white business man; and thus, by the rigid laws of custom, he has continually lost golden opportunities to forge his fortune; yet he has prospered in spite of this, and it bespeaks for him a superior manhood.

CHAPTER XXX.

RELIGIOUS PROGRESS.

BEFORE the war, the colored people of the South worshipped mainly in the white churches, or in separate churches usually ministered to by white pastors. But the colored people, naturally inclined to religion, soon developed preachers of their own. They composed their own music, which expressed, in their own way, thanks and petitions to heaven. Their music is original, entertaining, and pathetic—and the only original music of the American Continent, when we remember that other than Negro techniques and melodies are all borrowed from the masters of Europe.

Debarred of the Privileges of schools, it is not surprising that the religion of the slaves should be otherwise than somewhat twisted from the cultured tone of the Bible to suit the whims of an unlettered race. It can be truly said though, that, considering the circumstances, they did not bury the talents given them. But the religious progress since free-**dom** is so marvellous as to completely overshadow much of the darkness of the past. Let us notice briefly several of the great religious denominations of the race. The colored people produce less infidels than any other similar number of people in America. They are proverbially religious and God-fearing.

Bishop W. J. Gaines.

Bishop W. J. Gaines is a representative of what twenty-five years of freedom has done in many instances for the colored race. He was born a slave in Georgia on the plantation of the famous Robert Toombs, member of the Confederate Cabinet.. He had reached his majority before the war ended, and it is needless to say his chances for early culture were very meagre. But, nevertheless, he learned to read at odd moments, and after freedom applied himself to his books with undaunted and determined zeal. He often speaks of how "I made up my mind when I entered the ministry to reach the highest position in my church through merit." He has won his coveted prize in this respect; and each step of his life, from the plow-handle to the Bishopric, has been markedly illustrious. He is a living argument of the innate genius of the race, that might, like the poet's rose, have been " born to blush unseen," but for the fact that he embraced the possibilities that freedom opened up before him. He is of commanding presence, dignified, and a natural leader of men. It is an inspiration to be in his presence, and his appearance on the rostrum is natural and complete.

He has possibly built more church edifices than any other member of his denomination. Morris Brown College, of Atlanta, worth something over seventy thousand dollars, is the work of his hands, and that of itself would sufficiently speak for his ability, without referring to thousands of dollars raised for other purposes. Bishop Gaines can be counted on to foster and encourage any enterprise tending to the benefit of the Negro race, and, he never fails to encourage the young people who are anxious to rise.

The A. M. E. Church, founded by Rev. Richard Allen, of Philadelphia, Penn., because of the spirit of caste and race prejudice of the Protestant Church during and after the American Revolution, has exerted a broad and unmeasured influence upon the Negro race. From a meeting held in 1816, at Rev. Allen's private house, has sprung surprising results. It has 3394 churches, valued at $5,028,126; 660 parsonages, valued at $312,763.75, and the total valuation of church property is $5,341,889.25. It has a publication department, which sends out the *Christian Recorder* and *A. M. E. Review* to thousands of people. The salaries of the editors of these papers amount to $10,800. In 1887, the money raised for all purposes was $1,064,569.50, with an indebtedness of $509,113.24. Wilberforce University is a noted institution controlled by the A. M. E. Church. The influence of this church for good among the people cannot be measured. The bishops are an extraordinary set of learned men, many of whom are self-made, but yet are authors, orators, linguists, theologians and scholars that will compare favorably with the best theological brain of America.

Rev. E. M. Brawley, of Charleston, S. C., is noted especially for his sober, earnest and pious Christian life. He is a scholarly gentleman, and

Rev. E. M. Brawley.

thoroughly devoted to the interests of his people. It has been his fortune to be President of Selma University, Ala.; Sunday-school agent in South Carolina, and editor of the *Baptist Tribune.* Such a hard-working, zealous and thoroughly honest man should be a pride to any race.

The Baptist Church was founded by Roger Williams. The church officers derive their power **from the members.** In the beginning, Roger Williams' influence had a tendency to keep down race prejudice. But from the rapid increase of slaves, the feeling grew until self-interest demanded a separation. They form a body of useful and intelligent people. Kentucky has a host of Baptists, who own much valuable property. There are more Baptists in Virginia than in any other Southern State. Some of the churches have very large congregations. There are a large number of Baptist churches in the District of Columbia, some of which have interesting histories. Among the noble, true and faithful workers of the Baptists are Duke, Williams, Anderson, and Leonard, Andrew Grimes and Dr. W. J. Simmons (deceased), of Louisville, Ky., who have consecrated their lives to their church in the spreading of the Gospel.

The Baptist Church exercises a religious and educational influence over more colored people than any other denomination in America. I gather from the minutes of their National Convention of 1887, that they have a total membership in the United States of 1,155,486; and that they have 6605 ordained ministers, 3304 Sabbath-schools with 10,718 teachers and officers and 194,492 pupils. They own $3,056,571 worth of church property. They operate twenty-five colleges and seminaries, worth $1,072-140, and in which are annually taught more than 3609 pupils.

The A. M. E. Zion Church is another of the powerful religious denominations among the colored people, and is everywhere urging the race to a higher standard of living in all respects. Their membership is in the neighborhood of 500,000. They support and control, entirely, Livingston College, of Salisbury, N. C., a progressive and well-manned institution, and the *Star of Zion*, the church organ, ably edited by Mr. John C. Dancy. The Livingston College Faculty is all colored, and it has property valued at over $100,000.

The Northern Methodist Church supports many churches in the South ministered over by colored pastors. There are several schools supported by them, prominent among which is Bennet College of Greensboro, N. C., and controlled entirely by a colored Faculty. Other schools of this denomination, manned by white Faculties, are, with Bennet College, doing a most necessary and beneficial work among the colored people. So might be mentioned schools and churches supported by Northern Presbyterians, Northern Congregationalists, Episcopalians, and other denominations, all of which are to be reckoned as great uplifting agencies among the colored people. Some of the Northern societies spend hundreds of thousands of dollars every year on Negro education and religion in the South. The *daily* expenditure of the American

Livingston College.

Missionary Association for schools and churches in the South is estimated at $1200.

The Presbyterian Church has not spread as rapidly among the Negroes as some other forms of belief, and yet within the past twenty-five years that church has taken a strong hold among them, chiefly in Virginia, the Carolinas, Georgia, Florida, and Tennessee. Within the territory embraced in these States, there are 2 Synods, 10 Presbyteries, 200 ministers, 250 churches, 18,000 communicants, and 15,000 Sabbath-school scholars. Except twelve or fifteen ministers, and a few score members, these synods are composed of Negroes, who control the affairs of the churches and schools. They are in ecclesiastical fellowship with the Northern Presbyterian Church. Their organ is the *Africo-American Presbyterian*, published at Charlotte, N. C., by the Africo-American Presbyterian Publishing Company, with Rev. D. J. Sanders, D.D.,* as editor. This journal has a wide circulation.

Educational Work of the Presbyterians.— Under the auspices of the Presbyterians are Lincoln University, Oxford, Pennsylvania, which is their leading institution for educating colored men, and from which more Negro graduates have gone out, into all the professions and as ministers and teachers, into the different denominations, than from any similar school in the country; Biddle University,

---
* Dead.

Charlotte, N. C., ranking among the first in the South, now presided over by Rev. D. J. Sanders,* D.D., has an able Faculty of white and colored men; and the far-famed Scotia Seminary, at Concord, N. C., under the presidency of Rev. D. J. Satterfield,† D.D., with an able corps of teachers. Scotia Seminary has done, and is doing, much for the education of colored girls, and ranks second to none of the seminaries of its kind. The attendance last year was 240, and accommodations are being provided for 150 more.

* Dead.
† Retired.

CHAPTER XXXI.

EDUCATIONAL PROGRESS.

Can the Negro learn anything? was the first question he had to answer after schools were established for him.   He has answered this question satisfactorily to the most incredulous in every instance where brought to a test.   The fact that every slave State had laws against his being taught before the war, and that they opposed it afterwards, ought to be a sufficient answer.   But if this is not sufficient, let speak the deeds of Professor Scarborough, of Macon, Ga., author of a series of Greek text-books which have been adopted at Yale; George W. Williams, author of " History of the American Negro ;" Jos. T. Wilson, author of " Black Phalanx ;" C. G. Morgan, class orator at Harvard, 1890, and a host of others.

WHAT THE SOUTH IS DOING FOR NEGRO EDUCATION.

It would be a serious error to omit, in speaking of the educational progress of the Negro since freedom, what has been done to help him by the Southern States.   Though at first bitterly opposed to Negro education, there has been a wonderful change of sentiment on this subject.   They made laws against Negro education before the war, now they make laws for it. In the more liberal portions of many Southern States, good schools are provided for the colored children. Some States have asylums for the deaf, dumb, blind and insane. The Institute for these unfortunates at Raleigh, N. C., is entirely supported by the State. Texas has a similar school. The South spends annually about $6,000,000 on Negro schools, and this sum will soon be increased. Some of the States have Normal Schools, Universities and Training Schools for the colored youth. There are some who oppose Negro education on the ground that the whites pay two-thirds of the taxes. A false position this—the laborer and consumer pay the taxes on capital. The Negro is the laborer of the South, and a large consumer. He produces more than a billion dollars' worth of farm products annually, not estimating other products; and it is his toil, his muscle that makes the school-fund; and out of the inexhaustible store-house of his own labor does he draw his quota of the appropriation for the schools. Add also what he pays into the fund by taxes.

The High Schools, Seminaries, Colleges and Professional Schools for the colored people number nearly two hundred. Many of them are controlled entirely by colored Faculties, as Livingston and Bennett Colleges, N. C.; Morris Brown College, Ga.;

Tuskegee Normal School, Ala.; Wilberforce University, Ohio; Virginia Normal and Collegiate Institute; Kittrell's Normal and Industrial Institute, and Shaw University, except its President, who is white, but one of the first Presidents to recognize the ability of young colored men to teach the higher branches. Dr. H. M. Tupper* inaugurated a movement by putting young colored men at work in Shaw University, which has been followed by many of the other schools supported by donations from white friends in the North. The plan works admirably well, and, besides teaching the race to confide in the ability of its own educated men and women, it affords lucrative employment to many who are by nature and choice fitted for the work of teaching.

A Self-made Man is a worthy description when applied to a Saxon. But a knowledge of the facts will teach us that nine-tenths of all the leading Negroes were and are self-made. The royal road to knowledge is beyond question closed to the young colored man.

There is No Large Estate to draw on for school bills; no rich uncle or kinsman to foot the bill and wait till success in after years for a settlement. His own brawny muscle is usually the young colored student's means of support. Many of them work in school between hours. In fact, most of the

* Now dead.

Snaw University.

schools for colored people in the South assign certain hours each day in which the students are to
labor.   Some institutions do not spend one cent for
domestic labor during the whole of the school terms.
Yet they, in some instances, raise quite enough farm
and garden products for their tables, and sometimes
make brick enough to put up extra buildings.   The
time usually used by the white student in foot-ball
and other games is utilized by the colored student
in faithful toil.   The fact that in none of the colored
schools the expense for tuition, board, lodging, laun-
dry-work and incidentals is over $12 per month
(and in some cases it is as low as $6), is a strong
argument in favor of the help the Negro youth furnishes towards his own education.   People with
such a love for knowledge that they are willing to
thus toil for it, may be relied upon to use that
knowledge properly.

When the War Closed there were about four
million colored people in the United States.   Scarcely
a million of them could read.   Now they number
about eight millions, and nearly half of them can
read.   There are 1,158,008 colored children in the
schools, annually taught by 20,000 Negro teachers.
The colored people of the South have made more
progress in education since the war than in anything
else; and they are still thirsty for knowledge.   The
schools everywhere are crowded.   The love of
knowledge seems to be instinctive, and thousands of

faithful mothers spend many weary nights at the ironing-board and wash-tub in order to get money to help their children obtain an education. With the start they now have, twenty-five years more of earnest work will show marvellous changes in the educational condition of the race No people ever learned more in so short a time.

MUSICAL PROGRESS.

The Fisk Jubilee Singers have sung the fame of the Negro in all America, much of Europe and Australia. The slave music is the only original music of America. The Indian has none, and white Americans have borrowed from the masters of Europe. Negro melodies are now a part of the *classical* music of this country. The peculiarity of Negro song is its pathos and trueness to nature. It stirs the soul and revives a sunken hope. Travellers describe the music of the native African as sung in a *major* key, which key characterizes the songs of a conquering people. Slavery has not extracted this characteristic totally from the American Negro's songs. While he sings not the conquering *major* of battle, he thrills you with the pleasing *minor* of hope. Dr. Talmage says: " Everybody knows the natural gift of the African for singing. No singing on this continent like that of the colored churches in the South. Everybody going to Richmond or Charleston wants to hear the Africans sing."

CHAPTER XXXII.

FINANCIAL PROGRESS.

The Freedmen's Savings Bank, though it failed, furnishes a strong argument in favor of the thrift and industry of the recently emancipated slaves. In this bank the colored people deposited during the years between 1866 and 1871, about $57,000,000. The original design of this institution was doubtless good, but it fell into bad hands, and the consequence was a most disgraceful failure.

The Negro's Confidence in banks was, on his first trial of them, badly shaken. He has not recovered yet. Many colored people who would deposit their money now, are reluctant to do so when they remember the "Freedmen's Bank failure." The branch offices of the bank in the different States were placed in the hands of colored men who worked for salaries under instructions from the home office. To this day sentiment attaches blame on these colored bank officers, who themselves were as much deluded as the depositors. It was a sad and disgraceful piece of legalized robbery. But the Negro is *putting his money in other enterprises,* and though unsuccessful in his first, his last efforts at economy are bearing rich fruit. The property owned by the colored people now is computed at the following figures:

Twenty-five Years' Accumulations : Alabama, $9,200,125 ; Arkansas, $8,010,315 ; Florida, $7,900,400 ; Georgia, $10,415,330 ; Kentucky, $5,900,010 ; Louisiana, $18,100,528 ; Mississippi, $13,400,213 ; Missouri, $6,600,343 ; North Carolina, $11,010,652 ; South Carolina, $12,500,000 ; Texas, $18,010,545 ; Tennessee, $10,400,211 ; Virginia, $4,900,000.

The Colored Churches in the United States own $16,310,441 ; the total amount of property owned by the colored people in *all* the States is rated at over $263,000,000.*

Much Property is owned by the colored people of the North and West. Some of their estates run high into the hundred thousands. Many of them, though shut out almost entirely from the trades and business avenues, have accumulated handsome homes, and live in elegance and refinement.

Rev. A. G. Davis, of Raleigh, N. C., in an address at the North Carolina Colored Agricultural Fair, said, in reference to the Negro's progress, this, among other things : " Scan, if you will, the long line of eight million Negroes as they march slowly but surely up the road of progress, and you will find in her ranks such men as Granville T. Woods, of

* It is now estimated that the figures in this paragraph may be doubled.

Ohio, the electrician, mechanical engineer, manufac-
turer of telephones, telegraph and electrical instruments; William Still, of Philadelphia, the coal-
dealer; Henry Tanner, the artist; John W. Terry,
foreman of the iron and fitting department of the
Chicago West Division Street Car Company; J. D.
Baltimore, engineer, machinist, and inventor, of
Washington, D. C.; Wiley Jones, of Pine Bluff,
Ark., the owner of a street car railroad, race-track,
and park; Richard M. Hancock, foreman of the
pattern shops of the Eagle Works and Manufac-
turing Co., and draughtsman; John Black, the inventor, whose inventions are worth tens of thousands; W. C. Atwood, the lumber merchant and
capitalist."

All the States have numbers of colored individuals whose wealth is rated between five and ten
thousand dollars.

In closing this chapter on the progress of the
race since the war, we desire to say to you, our
young readers, that much has been done, as you
have read in this chapter, to raise the race in the
estimation of the world, but much more remains
to be done. What has been said in this chapter is
not to make you content and satisfied, but rather,
to inspire new zeal and fresh courage, that each
one of you may add something more to what has
already been accomplished. You can, you must,

and we believe you will. Do not falter on account of difficulties. Set your standard high and go to it, remembering that labor, coupled with a strong devotion to integrity, will surely conquer.

CHAPTER XXXIII.

SOME NOTED NEGROES.

Hon. Hiram R. Revels, a native of North Carolina, graduate of Knox College, Ill., A. M. E. minister, President of Alcorn University, Mississippi, elected to the State Senate, Mississippi, was the first Negro to hold the position of U. S. Senator, elected to fill the place of Jefferson Davis in 1869, to the wonder and surprise of all America.

Hon. J. Mercer Langston, A.B., A.M., LL.D.; great Indian-Anglo-Saxon Negro. Grew to manhood, educated and pursued a business and official life in Ohio up to time of manhood. He made unsuccessful attempts, on account of his color, in New York and Ohio, to attend the law schools. After attempting private lessons, he grew discouraged and graduated from the Theological Department of Oberlin College, Ohio. He then studied law and was admitted to the bar. After this he was made Dean and Professor of Law at Howard University, where he received the degree of LL.D. President Hayes appointed him U. S. Minister and Consul-General to Hayti, which position he honorably held eight years. He was also President of the Virginia Normal Collegiate Institute.

Hon. Robert Small, the pilot and captain of the steamer Planet, also the Congressman, must not be

Robert Small.

overlooked on these pages. Moving from Beaufort, South Carolina, to Charleston in '51, he was employed as " rigger," thereby getting a knowledge of ships and the life of sailors. His greatest work was with the Planter, a Confederate transport steamer in '61, afterwards used as a dispatch boat. The officers retired from the boat on the night of May 13, 1862, and left eight colored men on watch, Small being one of the number. He was only called a wheelman then, but in reality was a pilot. He with the others on board conceived the risky plan of giving the boat over to the Federals. Everything being ready, and after taking on Small's wife and three children, they started out at 2 o'clock. In passing out of the harbor and by each fort the steamer gave her signals as though the Confederate captain was on board, and everything was all right. The dangerous plan, which if it had been found out would have ended in instant death, was a success. The boat was given over to the Federal Captain Nichols, who found her quite an additional help to the Union.

ROBERT R. ELLIOTT.

On the pages of history no name shines forth with more lustre than that of Hon. Robert B. Elliott. He was one of earth's sons, plucked too soon to reap the harvest which was in store for him. This eloquent orator and distinguished lawyer was a graduate from an English college. After finishing there he studied law under Fitz-Herbert, of the London bar. He then came to the United States, and began his brilliant and successful career. It

was in the Forty-second Congress, while a representative of South Carolina, that he impressed him·
self indelibly upon the minds of his country as a
man of giant intellect and rare oratorical ability.
Alexander Stephens of Georgia, Beck of Kentucky,
Harris of Virginia, had severely assailed the constitutionality of the Civil Rights Bill, after which
Mr. Elliott arose and addressed the House as follows, an effort that bespeaks the ability of the man:
" Mr. Speaker, while I am sincerely grateful for the
high mark of courtesy that has been accorded me
by this House, it is a matter of regret to me that it
is necessary at this day that I should rise in the
presence of an American Congress to advocate a
bill which simply asserts rights and equal privileges
for all classes of American citizens. I regret, sir,
that the dark hue of my skin may lend a color to the
imputation that I am controlled by motives personal
to myself in my advocacy of this great measure of
natural justice. Sir, the motive that impels me is
restricted by no such narrow boundary, but is as
broad as your Constitution. I advocate it, sir, because it is right. The bill, however, not only appeals
to your justice, but it demands a response to your
gratitude. In the events that led to the achievement of American independence the Negro was not
an inactive or unconcerned spectator. He bore his
part bravely upon many battle-fields, although un-

cheered by that certain hope of political elevation
which victory would secure to the white man. The
tall granite shaft which a grateful State has reared
above its sons who fell in defending Fort Griswold
against the attack of Benedict Arnold, bears the
name of John Freeman and others of the African
race, who there cemented with their blood the corner-
stone of your Republic. In the State which I have
had the honor in part to represent, the rifle of the
black man rang out against the troops of the British
crown in the darkest days of the American Revolution. . . . . I meet him (Stephens) only as an ad-
versary, nor shall age or any other consideration
restrain me from saying that he now offers this
Government, which he has done his utmost to destroy, a very poor return for its magnanimous treatment, to come here to seek to continue, by the assertion of doctrines obnoxious to the true principles
of our Government, the burdens and oppressions,
which rest upon five millions of his countrymen who
never failed to lift their earnest prayers for the success of this Government, when the gentleman was
asking to break up the Union of the States, and to
blot the American Republic from the galaxy of nations." . . . . He related to Mr. Beck the story of
the fleeing of the Kentucky soldiers at a most urgent
time during the second war with Great Britain,
and then proceeded to say: "In quoting this indis-

putable piece of history, I do so only by way of ad-monition, and not to question the well-attested gal-lantry of the true Kentuckian, and to suggest to the gentleman that *he* should not flaunt his heraldry so proudly while he bears this bar-sinister on the mili-tary escutcheon of his State—a State which answered the call of the Republic in 1861, when treason thun-dered at the very gates of the capital, by coldly de-claring her neutrality in the impending struggle. The Negro, true to that patriotism that has ever characterized and marked his history, came to the aid of the Government in its efforts to maintain the Constitution.   To that Government he now appeals; that Constitution he now invokes for protection against unjust prejudices founded upon caste."

William Wells Brown, Esq., was born of slave parents; he escaped to the North and so im-proved his time from then on, until he is now known to the world as M.D.; historian of the Negro race, lecturer and author.

Rev. D. A. Payne, D.D., LL.D., is the oldest bishop of the A. M. E. Church, also its true, tried friend. He is a great educator, and has the Negro's best interests at heart; many generous and noble deeds has he done for his race; he is the scholar and reverenced father of the A. M. E. Church.

Rev. William T. Dixon, the pastor of Concord Baptist Church, greatly deserves notice. Rev. Dixon

Bishop D. A. Payne.

has been a great power in his church, and has been the means of exerting an excellent intellectual and moral influence upon his people at Brooklyn, N. Y. His efforts for the conversion of the souls of his fellow-men are untiring, patient, and full of sacrifice. Many faces brighten and hearts ring with joy when his name is called.

Bishop H. M. Turner, D.D., is well known throughout the United States; he stands as a model for the poor boy to-day with scanty means. His early efforts for an education were accompanied with many disappointments and failures. Though free, he had to submit to the law, "no Negro must be educated." However, he got a start and added to his small stock until he could read the Bible and hymn-book. It is said that he learned fifty psalms in a night, and while plowing repeated them to his co-laborers. He was hired out most of the time by his father; his work was always with hard and often cruel overseers; but he said, and kept his word, when a boy, no white man should whip and scar his back. When about fifteen years of age he was employed as waiting-boy in a law office, where he attracted special notice by his tenacious memory and accuracy in delivering messages; the lawyers took an interest in him and taught him whatever he wanted to learn. From this he moved on, from one level to the next higher—being a hard student all the way up to the present. He now is known as bishop, philosopher, politician, author, devoted, race-man, and ex-United States Chaplain.

Hon. P. B. S. Pinchback has the honor of having held more positions than any other colored man. He was a true and faithful soldier during the civil war. At the time of the impeachment of Governor Warmouth, of Louisiana, he became acting Governor of that State, finally becoming the real Governor until the term expired.

Prof. Richard Theodore Greener stands with the first scholars of the Negro race. His essays and orations rank high in the fields of literature and oratory. He has held the position of Chief Civil Service Examiner of New York City, lawyer, prize essayist, orator, and Dean o the Law Department of Howard University.

Senator B. K. Bruce, another son of the Negro race, though not receiving his privilege as a man until 1865, and notwithstanding then having attained to the age of 24, smothered no longer the intellectual fires then burning in his soul. Though a Virginian, he entered into public life in Mississippi. Much useful knowledge he gathered while sergeant-at-arms of the State Senate of Mississippi, which helped him to admirably fill his place as U. S. Senator. It was, also, his honor to hold the position of Register of the U. S. Treasury.

B. K. Bruce.

Prof. W. S. Scarborough is the author of
a set of Greek text-books; he is also versed
in many of the modern and ancient languages, including Gothic, Zend, Old Slavonic,
Lithuanian and Sanscrit. In every respect he is
a representative man, having come up from pov-
erty and obscurity to his present high position

in life. He was born in Macon, Ga. When the war closed he, like many other colored boys, entered the "Yankee school" there, from which he subsequently attended Atlanta University; from there he went to Oberlin, Ohio, where he graduated in 1875. He taught school in the vacation months to support himself while in school. Well may we say he is a self-made man, if unflagging industry, self-reliance, and an indomitable determination to succeed may be counted as ingredients in the make-up of such characters. He is now the President of Wilberforce University, which position he holds in preference to many others his scholarly abilities fit him for, and which he might attain. He is recognized as a thorough scholar by the world of learned men, and stands out as an unchallenged vindication of the race's ability.

Prof. B. T. Washington is what we so often hear of, a self-made man. Being left quite young an orphan, to forge his own way through the world, he started out determined to get an education. With the assistance of friends he reached Hampton Institute with fifty cents in his pocket. He finished the course by working out his expenses as janitor. After graduating at Hampton, he taught a while at Malden, Va., then his home, and then took a course of study at Wayland Seminary. He taught two years at Hampton Institute, and then accepted the position of Principal of the Tuskegee Normal School, which he has held with a remarkable degree of success and honor to himself and his race.   The school is now in a flourishing condition, and doing much good throughout the State of Alabama, and even in other States.

Prof. E. E. Smith, a native North Carolinian, and a young man of the *post-bellum* school, has quickly risen to fame by an appointment under President Cleveland as Minister' of the U. S. Goverment to the Republic of Liberia. Mr. Smith served in this position for four years with honor and credit to himself and his country.   Prior to his appointment as Minister to Liberia, he was the worthy Principal of the Fayetteville, N. C., Normal School. He is a graduate of the famous Shaw University, and destined to reflect still greater honors on this his *Alma Mater*.

Rev. J. C. Price, D.D., the well-known temperance orator, lives in the hearts of many people. His clear and distinct voice, fascinating manner and excellent ability to handle a story, gave him a hearty welcome in every place to which he went. He was the first colored preacher to stand in the pulpit of Henry Ward Beecher, and then with the sympathy and love of a parent for his pupils, he with honor held the position of President of Livingston College, North Carolina.   He was a native of North Carolina.

J. C. Price.

EDMONIA LEWIS.

The subject of this sketch, by the diligent use of the powers God gave her, has done much to demonstrate to the world what genius exists in the race she represents. Left an orphan in early life, she was not educated according to her desire, but was conscious of a power and a burning zeal to make herself felt in the world.

Her first visit to Boston proved the turning point in her life. When she for the first time saw the statue of Franklin her soul was touched. While the dull stone seemed cold to others, there was a chord in her young soul which the cold lineaments played upon, and she exclaimed exultingly, "I can make a stone man." Wm. Lloyd Garrison, always ready to help the race, introduced her to a leading Boston sculptor. He gave her some clay and a model of a human foot, saying, "Go home and make that; if there is anything in you it will come out." Her first effort was brought back to the teacher, who examined it, then broke it to pieces, telling her to try again. She did so, and succeeded. Her achievements since have placed her among the prominent artists of the world. She now resides at Rome, where her studio is the famed resort of art-lovers the world over. Some of her works are, busts of Charles Sumner, Lincoln, Hiawatha's Wooing, Forever Free, Hagar in the Wilderness, Madonna with Infant Christ, and two Adoring Angels. She was patronized by the leading Englishmen, such as D'Israeli, and others.

T. T. Fortune, Esq., the well-known and fearless editor, was also a slave, born of slave parents, in Florida. He is a deep thinker, and an enthusiastic and true worker for his race. A great agitator and denouncer of the wrong and encourager of the right; also an author and pamphleteer.

Rev. W. J. Simmons, A.M., D.D., was, beyond question, one of the strongest characters of the race. He was the President of the Normal and Theological Institute at Louisville, Ky. At one time he was editor of the *American Baptist*, and did a telling work in that position by his strong editorials and telling points in behalf of the interests of the race. But Rev. Simmons is better known as an educator. He took charge of the Institute at Louisville when nothing but failure seemed to stare it in the face; and from an appearance of hopeless ruin he has worked it up to a point of great excellency. It now stands as one of the most important factors of Negro education in the South, and its success is due to the indomitable energy, force, and brain of Dr. Simmons. He has also furnished the literature of the race with a valuable work known as " Men of Mark." In it you will be pleased to read elegant sketches f many of the race's best men.

The Hon. H. P. Cheatham is a son of Shaw University, and a young man whose success is due to emancipation. He was for eight years a member of Congress, having won his seat through a desperate contest for the Second District of North Carolina. His record in Congress is good; not so much known, however, for his " much speaking," as for the devotion he shows to the interests of his race. Mr. Cheatham came up from the ranks of the school teachers, leaving off that work to take a position as Register of Deeds in his (Vance) county, which position he held creditably for a number of years, and which he resigned to run for Congress in 1888.

John R. Lynch.

Hon. John R. Lynch is another son of whom we may be proud. He hid not his talents, but rather multiplied them. It was his honor to preside at the National Republican Convention in 1884, at Chicago.

We know him as orator, lawyer, Congressman, prominent politician and paymaster in the U. S. Army.

Among the Noted Singers should be mentioned Madame Selika, "the colored Jenny Lind." Her voice is, perhaps, sweeter than the renowned Jenny Lind (white), and capable of greater variation in length and pitch. Madame Selika stands as a prodigy among singers. She would stand near the head of modern female voices were it not that she is colored.

Mrs. Frances Ellen Harper, a native of Baltimore, Maryland, was denied the opportunities of an education in her early days, but as soon as the way was opened she applied herself with such energy and earnestness as to develop her rare intellectual abilities, and put her before the world as a grand, good woman. She is known as an entertaining lecturer and pleasing essayist.

Miss Flora Batson Bergen was another representative of the art of song. The wonder is that she rendered the most difficult classical music from memory, being unable to read notes. She was an undoubted genius.

Miss H. Q. Brown stands high as an elocutionist, and reader of wonderful force and descriptive powers. Her work compares favorably with any of the kind in America, and her reputation is national.

Miss Ednorah Nahar, of Boston, Mass., has achieved wonderful results as a reader and elocutionist. She is yet young in the work, but has read in nearly all of the leading cities in America and Canada, and received the highest encomiums from the best dramatical critics in both countries, one of whom says; " Her art is no art, but Nature itself."

Blind Tom.

"Blind Tom," the Negro Musical Prodigy, is known as well in Europe as America. His cor· rect name is Thomas Bethune. He was born May

25, 1849, at Columbus, Georgia. When a babe he
seemed totally blind, but in later years he could see
a little. His memory of dates, persons and places
seems almost perfect. Shake his hand to-day and
speak to him, tell your name, and ten years after he
will recall your voice and name. He is uniformly
and studiously polite, and entertains the highest regard for truth in all things. At four years of age
he found his way to his master's piano for the first
time. He had attempted to use his voice in imitat-
ing the piano and other sounds before this. He
imitated all the sounds he knew on the piano, and
when his supply was exhausted he began to com-
pose for himself. He would play, as he would remark, "*what the wind said*," or the "*birds said*," or
the '*trees said*." When five years old, during a
thunder-storm, he composed his "*Rain Storm*,"
which is so true to Nature that one imagines on
hearing it that he can hear the thunder roar, and
"looks for the lightning to flash." One author says
of him: "I can't teach him anything; he knows
more of music than we know or can know. We
can learn all that great genius can reduce to rule
and put in tangible form ; he knows more than that.
I do not even know what it is; but I feel it is something beyond my comprehension. All that can be
done for him will be to let him hear fine playing;
he will work it all out for himself after awhile."

He plays the most difficult classical music of Mendelssohn and Beethoven, and cannot read a note. His marches include "Delta Kappa Epsilon," by Peace; "Grand March de Concert," by Wallace. He imitates as perfectly as if natural, "Battle of Manassas," "Douglass' Speech," guitar, banjo, church organ, Dutch woman and hand-organ, a harp, Scotch bagpipe, and a music-box—all on the piano. His equal, if it ever existed in the world, has not been known. He stands out as a phenomenon, a genius, a prodigy in black. He still lives, and is constantly improving and adding to his large stock of musical achievements.*

Toussaint L'Ouverture.—It is supposed that L Ouverture was born in 1743, in San Domingo, on " All Saints' Day," from which he was named Toussaint. The name L'Ouverture was given him after he had won a high place in the army by many brilliant conquests. He was born a slave, and said to be a direct descendant of an African king. He was educated by his god-father, Pierre Baptiste. Later he had an interesting family, and was as happy as a slave could be. He believed himself destined to lead his race out of bondage. Having access to his master's library, he read much; and it is recorded that he always mastered whatever work he undertook to study. It is generally conceded by his enemies that he was honest, honorable, and just. On

---

* Thomas Bethune is now reported to be dead.

the night of August 21, 1791, the revolution which
was destined to free the blacks of Hayti began. It
was, really, the culmination of a series of political

Toussaint L'Ouverture.
" Soldier—Statesman—Martyr." — *Wendell Phillips.*

struggles which had been waged with fury between
the government of France, the white planters, and
the mulattoes who thought that they were entitled to

equal political privileges with the whites. This point
was bitterly contested by the whites of the colony,
until the mulattoes succeeded in inciting the blacks
to murder and pillage. Toussaint took no part in
the murderous proceedings of this night, and did
not leave the plantation until he had safely provided
for all the whites thereon, whom he afterwards had
conveyed to Baltimore. He was always opposed to
a general massacre of the whites, and throughout
his career, as a commander, exerted his influence
to preserve their lives. Upon entering military life
his promotion was rapid, as he possessed all the
requisites of a great commander and leader. Having risen to a generalship, because of his many suc-
cesses, France acknowledged his rank and tendered
to him a commission as commander-in-chief of the
armies of San Domingo, in 1797. There followed
three years of unparalleled prosperity, during which
time L'Ouverture's ability as a statesman and ruler
was shown to great advantage. Napoleon, however, became jealous of L'Ouverture's power, and the
old troubles in Hayti being renewed, they declared
their independence in 1801. Napoleon sent large
armies to the island, but they all failed to conquer
the brave band of blacks under their indomitable
leader, Toussaint. Finally, they resorted to strata-
gem. They pretended to make peace, after which
Toussaint was invited on one occasion to dine on

board a French man-of-war, and there he was captured, sent to France, confined in a dark, damp dun-
geon, and allowed to die of hunger. He died in
1803, heroically proclaiming that though the French
might murder him, the tree of liberty would still
grow in San Domingo; how unlike Napoleon, the
author of Toussaint's torture, who ended *his* existence in writing and fretting on the island of St.
Helena, in similar confinement, a just retribution, it
seems, in atonement for the wrong he had done
L'Ouverture !

" His life lay in thought and in action rather than
in words. Self-contained, he was also self-sufficing.
Though he disdained not the advice of others, he
was, in the main, his own council-board. With an
intense concentration of vitality in his own soul, he
threw into his outer life a power and an energy
which armed one man with the power of thousands,
and made him great alike in command of others
and in command of himself. He was created for
government by the hand of nature. That strength
of soul and self reliance which made him fit to rule,
also gave him subjects for his sway. Hence it was,
that he could not remain in the herd of his fellow-
slaves. Rise he must, and rise he did; first to
humble offices, then to the command of a regiment,
and then to the command of the armies of San Domingo.'

CHAPTER XXXIV.

THE FREE PEOPLE OF COLOR IN NORTH CAROLINA.

BY THE HON. JOHN S. LEARY.

In the Revolutionary War there were enlisted as soldiers in the American army quite a number of colored men who served faithfully and fought gallantly for the cause of American Independence. Among others who enlisted from North Carolina, were Louie Revels, John Lomax, Thomas Bell, Charles Hood and John Pettiford. All of these surviving the contest drew, as long as they lived, a pension from the United States Government. When the Congress of freemen (*freeholders*) assembled at Halifax, and on the 18th day of December, 1776, ratified a Constitution for North Carolina, the elective franchise was extended to every freeman residing in the State who was twenty-one years of age and had paid a public tax. Under the provisions of this Constitution all free colored persons living in North Carolina who were twenty-one years of age and had paid a public tax, claimed and exercised the right to vote until the year 1835, a period of more than a half century, when the Convention which assembled that year, acting on the principle that might makes right, adopted an amended Constitution which barred them of that right. Having been barred of the right to vote by the provisions of the Constitution of 1835, in the year 1838 the question as to whether they were or were not citizens coming before the State Supreme Court, the following extract from the opinion of the Court, delivered by Gaston, Judge, will show that the Court decided that they were citizens:

"Whatever distinctions may have existed in the Roman law between citizens and free inhabitants, they are unknown to our institutions. Before our Revolution, all free persons born within the dominion of the King of Great Britain, whatever their color or complexion, were native-born British subjects—those born out of his allegiance were aliens. Slavery did not exist in England, but it did exist in the British Colonies. Slaves were not, in legal parlance, persons, but property. The moment the incapacity—or disqualification—of slavery was removed, they became persons, and were then either British subjects or not British subjects according as they were or were not born within the allegiance of the British King. Upon the close of the Revolution, no other change took place in the law of North

Carolina than was consequent upon the transition from a colony dependent on a European king to a free and sovereign State. Slaves remained slaves. British subjects in North Carolina became North Carolina freemen. Foreigners, until made citizens of the State, continued aliens. Slaves manumitted here became freemen—and, therefore, if born within North Carolina, are citizens of North Carolina—and all free persons born within the State are born citizens of the State."

However, under the provisions of the amended Constitution, and the laws enacted subsequent to its ratification by the Legislature, there existed in North Carolina, prior to the year 1865, three distinct classes of people: The free white man, enjoying and exercising all the rights and privileges of an American citizen; the free colored man, deprived of nearly all the rights and privileges of an American citizen; and, the colored slave, who, in legal parlance, was a mere chattel. Owing to this anomalous state of affairs, whatever was accomplished by the genius, industry, effort, culture, and literary attainments of the colored American residing in the State, was studiously ignored and cast aside as not worthy to be recorded as a part and parcel of the history of the people of the State.

To preserve the memory, as well as to perpetuate the work and worth of a very eminent colored citizen of North Carolina, I here present for the information of the youths, and all other persons who do not know anything of the history of his life, a biographical narrative of the Rev. John Chavers. This gentleman, a regularly ordained minister of the Presbyterian Church, came to the United States in the year 1822. He settled in North Carolina, and after remaining here for the period of time required by law, was naturalized and became a citizen of the State and United States. In culture and literary attainments he far excelled a majority of all classes of the people living in the State at that day and date. A Christian gentleman, possessing all the qualities which go to make a true and noble man, he was honored for his eminent ability, and respected for his Christian character. He lived in the town of Fayetteville for a period of two years, preached and taught school. He removed from Fayetteville, and afterwards lived respectively in the counties of Franklin, Wake, and Chatham, in each of which he preached and taught school. The school organized and taught by him in Chatham County was patronized almost exclusively by the white people. In the light of present surroundings, it may seem strange and incredulous that the white people of North Carolina would send their children to a colored school teacher, and consent to have their lives and characters shaped and moulded by him. But this is accounted for in the fact that the recorded history of those times goes to show that classical scholars and thoroughly equipped school teachers were not near so plentiful among the white people then as they are now, and they were not so very particular as to the color of the " Gamaliel " at whose feet their children should sit, provided he had the ability and learning to impart the desired information. As evidence of this gentleman's eminence as an instructor, and the influence which his precept and example had upon the lives and character of his pupils, I mention the names of a few who were so fortunate as to enjoy the benefit of his instruction and careful training. *The late Honorable Kenneth Rayner*, one of his pupils, was well known to the people of North Carolina as an eminent lawyer, and, before the civil war, as a representative from North Carolina in the United States Congress, and after said war was the able and efficient Solicitor-General of the United States Treasury under President Arthur's administration. Mr. Thos. J. Curtis, a successful business man, and for several years Mayor of the town of Fayetteville, was another ; and yet another was the late Honorable Abram Rencher, of Chatham County, who was one of the most distinguished men the State has ever produced. There were a great many others, but it is not necessary to mention by name any more.

These are enough to show that if justice had been done, this illustrious colored gentleman would have had a place in the recorded history of the State of his adoption as one of her earliest, most successful educators and eminent men.

CHAPTER XXXV

CONCLUSION.

Up to the present time the Negro has been a success in every avenue of life. As a soldier and citizen he has always been faithful to his country's flag; as a politician, he has filled successfully many honorable positions, from that of a Town Constable to the Registry of the Treasury of the United States; he has been a legislator, a senator, a judge, a lawyer, a juror, a shrewd business man, and won honor, respect, and confidence in every such position, and all this in twenty-five years. Every sort of hindrance has been thrown in his way, but he is overcoming them all, and daily winning friends from the ranks of those most opposed to his progress. Time is yet to bring forth better things for the race. Let there be patience, and an honest, persistent endeavor to do the very best in everything, and ere long we shall "reap if we faint not." We shall rise, not by dragging others down, but by encouraging those who are up to extend down to us the helping hand, which we must quickly grasp, and by its help *lift ourselves up.*

PART TWO

History of Negro Soldiers

IN THE SPANISH-AMERICAN WAR
AND OTHER ITEMS OF INTEREST

William McKinley.

HISTORY OF THE NEGRO SOLDIERS

IN THE SPANISH-AMERICAN WAR
AND OTHER ITEMS OF INTEREST

CHAPTER I.

THE CAUSE OF THE WAR WITH SPAIN.

Many Causes led up to the Spanish-American war. Cuba had been in a state of turmoil for a long time, and the continual reports of outrages on the people of the island by Spain greatly aroused the Americans. The "ten years' war" had terminated, leaving the island much embarrassed in its material interests, and woefully scandalized by the methods of procedure adopted by Spain and principally carried out by Generals Campos and Weyler, the latter of whom was called the "butcher" on account of his alleged cruelty in attempting to suppress the former insurrection. There was no doubt much to complain of under his administration, for which the General himself was not personally responsible. He boasted that he only had three individuals put to death, and that in each of these cases he was highly justified by martial law.

Finally the Attention of the United States was

forcibly attracted to Cuba by the Virginius affair, which consisted in the wanton murder of fifty American sailors—officers and crew of the Virginius, which was captured by the Spanish off Santiago bay, bearing arms and ammunition to the insurgents—Captain Fry, a West Point graduate, in command.

Spain would, no doubt, have received a genuine American thrashing on this occasion had she not been a republic at that time, and President Grant and others thought it unwise to crush out her republican principles, which then seemed just budding into existence.

The horrors of this incident, however, were not out of the minds of the American people when the new insurrection of 1895 broke out. At once, as if by an electric flash, the sympathy of the American people was enlisted with the Insurgents who were (as the Americans believed) fighting Spain for their **liberty.** Public opinion was on the Insurgents' side and against Spain from the beginning. This feeling of sympathy for the fighting Cubans knew no North nor South; and strange as it may seem the Southerner who quails before the mob spirit that disfranchises, ostracises and lynches an American Negro who seeks his liberty at home, became a loud champion of the Insurgent cause in Cuba, which was, in fact, the cause of Cuban Negroes and Mulattoes.

General Fitzhugh Lee, of Virginia, possibly

General Fitzhugh Lee.

the most noted Southerner of the day, was sent by President Cleveland to Havana as Consul General, and seemed proud of the honor of representing his government there, judging from his reports of the Insurgents, which were favorable. General Lee was retained at his post by President McKinley until it became necessary to recall him, thus having the high honor paid him of not being changed by the new McKinley administration, which differed from him in politics; and as evidence of General Fitzhugh Lee's sympathy with the Cubans it may be cited that he sent word to the Spanish Commander (Blanco) on leaving Havana that he would return to the island again and when he came he "would bring the stars and stripes in front of him."

Belligerent Rights to the Insurgents or Neutrality became the topic of discussion during the close of President Cleveland's administration. The President took the ground that the Insurgents, though deserving of proper sympathy, and such aid for humanity's sake as could be given them, yet they had not established on any part of the island such a form of government as could be recognized at Washington, and accorded belligerent rights or rights of a nation at war with another nation; that the laws of neutrality should be strictly enforced, and America should keep "hands off" and let Spain and the Insurgents settle their own differences.

Much Money and Time was expended by the United States government in maintaining this neutral position. Fillibustering expeditions were constantly being fitted up in America with arms and ammunition for the Cuban patriots. As a neutral power it became the duty of the American government to suppress fillibustering, but it was both an unpleasant and an expensive duty, and one in which the people had little or no sympathy.

Spain Tried to Appease public sentiment in America by recalling Marshal Campos, who was considered unequal to the task of defeating the Insurgents, because of reputed inaction. The flower of the Spanish army was poured into Cuba by the tens of thousands—estimated, all told, at three hundred thousand when the crisis between America and Spain was reached.

Weyler, "The Butcher," was put in command and inaugurated the policy of establishing military zones inside of the Spanish lines, into which the unarmed farmers, merchants, women and children were driven, penniless; and being without any visible means of subsistence were left to perish from hunger and disease. (The condition of these people greatly excited American sympathy with the Insurgents.) General Weyler hoped thus to weaken the Insurgents who received considerable of supplies from this class of the population, either by consent or force. Weyler's policy in reference to the reconcentrados (as these non-combatant people were called) rather increased than lessened the grievance, as was natural to suppose, in view of the misery and suffering it entailed on a class of people who most of all were not the appropriate subjects for his persecution, and sentiment became so strong in the United States against this policy (especially in view of the fact that General Weyler had promised to end the "Insurrection" in three months after he took command) that in

February, 1896, the United States Congress took up the discussion of the matter. Several Senators and Congressmen returned from visits to the island pending this discussion, in which they took an active and effective part, depicting a most shocking and revolting situation in Cuba, for which Spain was considered responsible; and on April 6th following this joint resolution was adopted by Congress:

"Be it Resolved by the Senate and House of Representatives of the United States of America, that in the opinion of Congress a public war exists between the Government of Spain and the Government proclaimed and for some time maintained by force of arms by the people of Cuba; and that the United States of America should maintain a strict neutrality between the contending powers, according to each all the rights of belligerents in the ports and territory of the United States.

"Resolved further, that the friendly offices of

the United States should be offered by the President to the Spanish government for the recognition of the independence of Cuba."

The Insurgents gained by this resolution an important point. It dignified their so-called insurrection into an organized army, with a government at its back which was so recognized and treated with. They could buy and sell in American ports.

General Antonio Maceo about this time was doing great havoc along the Spanish lines. He darted from place to place, back and forth across the supposed impassable line of Spanish fortifications stretching north and south across the island some distance from Havana, and known as the trocha. Thousands of Spaniards fell as the result of his daring and finesse in military execution. His deeds became known in America, and though a man of Negro descent, with dark skin and crisp hair, his fame was heralded far and wide in the American newspapers. At a public gathering in New York, where his picture was exhibited, the audience went wild with applause—the waving of handkerchiefs and the wild hurrahs were long and continued. The career of this hero was suddenly terminated by death, due to the treachery of his physician, Zertucha, who, under the guise of a proposed treaty of peace, induced him to meet a company of Spanish officers, at which meeting, according to a pre-arranged plot, a mob of Spanish infantry rushed

in on General Maceo and shot him down unarmed. It is said that his friends recovered his
body and buried it in a secret place unknown to
the Spaniards, who were anxious to obtain it for
exhibition as a trophy of war in Havana. Maceo
was equal to Toussaint L'Ouverture of San Domingo. His public life was consecrated to liberty; he knew no vice nor mean action; he would
not permit any around him. When he landed in
Cuba from Porto Rico he was told there were
no arms. He replied, "I will get them with my
machete," and he left five thousand to the
Cubans, conquered by his arm. Every time the
Spanish attacked him they were beaten and left
thousands of arms and much ammunition in his
possession. He was born in Santiago de Cuba
July 14, 1848.

The Spirit of the Insurgents did not break
with General Maceo's death. Others rose up to
fill his place, the women even taking arms in the
defence of home and liberty. "At first no one
believed, who had not seen them, that there were
women in the Cuban army; but there is no doubt
about it. They are not all miscalled amazons,
for they are warlike women and do not shun
fighting. The difficulty in employing them being that they are insanely brave. When they
ride into battle they become exalted and are dangerous creatures. Those who first joined the
forces on the field were the wives of men belonging in the army, and their purpose was rather to

General Antonio Maceo.

be protected than to become heroines and aven-
gers. It shows the state of the island, that the
women found the army the safest place for
them. With the men saved from the plantations and the murderous bandits infesting the
roads and committing every lamentable outrage
upon the helpless, some of the high-spirited
Cuban women followed their husbands, and the
example has been followed, and some, instead
of consenting to be protected, have taken up the
fashion of fighting."—Murat Halsted.

Jose Maceo, brother of Antonio, was also a
troublesome character to the Spaniards, who
were constantly being set upon by him and his
men.

Weyler's Policy and the Brave Struggle of the
people both appealed very strongly for American sympathy with the Insurgent cause. The
American people were indignant at Weyler and
were inspired by the conduct of the Insurgents.
Public sentiment grew stronger with every fresh
report of an Insurgent victory, or a Weyler
persecution.

Miss Evangelina Cosio y Cisneros' Rescue
helped to arouse sentiment. This young and
beautiful girl of aristocratic Cuban parentage
alleged that a Spanish officer had, on the occasion of a "raid" made on her home, in which her
father was captured and imprisoned as a Cuban
sympathizer, proposed her release on certain
illicit conditions, and on her refusal she was

incarcerated with her aged father in the renowned but filthy and dreaded Morro Castle at
Havana.

Appeal after Appeal by large numbers of the
most prominent women in America was made

Miss Evangelina Cosio y Cisneros.

to General Weyler, and even to the Queen Re-
gent of Spain, for her release, but without avail,
when finally the news was flashed to America
that she had escaped. This proved to be true

—her release being effected by Carl Decker, a reporter on the "New York Journal"—a most daring feat. Miss Cisneros was brought to America and became the greatest sensation of the day. Her beauty, her affection for her aged father, her innocence, and the thrilling events of her rescue, made her the public idol, and gave "Cuba libre" a new impetus in American sympathy.

Spain and Havana felt the touch of these ever spreading waves of public sentiment, and began to resent them. At Havana public demonstrations were made against America. The life of Consul General Lee was threatened. The Spanish Minister at Washington, Senor de Lome, was exposed for having written to a friend a most insulting letter, describing President McKinley as a low politician and a weakling. For this he was recalled by Spain at the request of the American government.

Protection to American citizens and property in Havana became necessary, and accordingly the **Battleship Maine** was sent there for this purpose, the United States government disclaiming any other motives save those of protection to Americans and their interests. The Maine was, to all outward appearances, friendly received by the Spaniards at Havana by the usual salutes and courtesies of the navy, and was anchored at a point in the bay near a certain buoy designated by the Spanish Commander. This was on January 25, 1898, and on February 15th this noble vessel was blown to pieces, and 266 of its crew perished—two colored men being in the number. This event added fuel to the already burning fire of American feeling against Spain. Public sentiment urged an immediate declaration of war. President McKinley counseled moderation. Captain Sigsbee, who survived the wreck

U.S.S. MAINE.

of the Maine, published an open address in which he advised that adverse criticism be delayed until an official investigation could be made of the affair.

The Official Investigation was had by a Court of Inquiry, composed of Captain W. T. Sampson of the Iowa, Captain F. C. Chadwick of the New York, Lieutenant-Commander W. P. Potter of the New York, and Lieutenant-Commander Adolph Marix of the Vermont, appointed by the President. Divers were employed; many witnesses were examined, and the court, by a unanimous decision, rendered March 21, 1898, after a four weeks' session, reported as follows: "That the loss of the Maine was not in any respect due to the fault or negligence on the part of any of the officers or members of her crew; that the ship was destroyed by the explosion of a submarine mine which caused the partial explosion of two or more of her forward magazines; and that no evidence has been obtainable fixing the responsibility for the destruction of the Maine upon any person or persons."

Responsibility in this Report is not fixed on any "person or persons." It reads something like the usual verdict of a coroner's jury after investigating the death of some colored man who has been lynched,—"he came to his death by the hands of parties unknown." This report on the Maine's destruction, "unlike" the usual coroner's jury verdict, however, in one respect, was not accepted by the people, who claimed that Spain was responsible, either directly or indirectly, for the explosion, and the public still clamored for war to avenge the outrage.

Congress also Caught the war fever and appropriated $50,000,000 "for the national defence" by a unanimous vote of both houses. The war and navy departments became very active; agents were sent abroad to buy war ships, but the President still hesitated to state his position until he had succeeded in getting the American Consuls out of Cuba who were in danger from the Spaniards there. Consul Hyatt embarked from Santiago April 3, and Consul General Lee, who was delayed in getting off American refugees, left on April 10, and on that day the **President sent his message to Congress.** He pictured the deplorable condition of the people of Cuba, due to General Weyler's policy; he recommended that the Insurgent government be not recognized, as such recognition might involve this government in "embarrassing international complications," but referred the whole subject to Congress for action.

Congress Declares War on April 13 by a joint resolution of the Foreign Affairs Committee of both houses, which was adopted, after a conference of the two committees, April 18, in the following form:

"Whereas, the abhorrent conditions which have existed for more than three years in the island of Cuba, so near our own borders, have shocked the moral sense of the people of the United States, have been a disgrace to Christian civilization, culminating as they have in the destruction of a United States battle ship, with 266 of its officers and crew, while on a friendly visit in the harbor of Havana, and cannot longer be endured, as has been set forth by the President of the United States in his message to Congress of April 11, 1898, upon which the action of Congress was invited: therefore,

"Resolved, by the Senate and House of Representatives of the United States of America in Congress assembled—

"First, that the people of the island of Cuba are, and of right ought to be, free and independent.

"Second, that it is the duty of the United States to demand, and the government of the United States does hereby demand, that the government of Spain at once relinquish its authority and government in the island of Cuba, and withdraw its land and naval forces from Cuba and Cuban waters.

"Third, that the President of the United States be, and he hereby is, directed and empowered to use the entire land and naval forces of the United States, and to call into the actual service of the United States the militia of the several States to such extent as may be necessary to carry these resolutions into effect.

"Fourth, that the United States hereby disclaims any disposition or intention to exercise sovereignty, jurisdiction or control over said island, except for the pacification thereof, and asserts its determination when that is completed to leave the government and control of the island to its people."

The President Signed this Resolution at 11:24

A. M. on the 20th of April, 1898. The Spanish Minister, Senor Luis Polo y Bernarbe, was served with a copy, upon which he asked for his passports, and "immediately left Washington."

"This is a picture of Edward Savoy, who accomplished one of the most signal diplomatic triumphs in connection with recent relations with Spain. It was he who outwitted the whole Spanish Legation and delivered the ultimatum to Minister Polo.

"Edward Savoy has been a messenger in the Department of State for nearly thirty years. He was appointed by Hamilton Fish in 1869, and held in high esteem by James G. Blaine.

"He was a short, squat, colored man, with a highly intelligent face, hair slightly tinged with gray and an air of alertness which makes him stand out in sharp contrast with the other messengers whom one meets in the halls of the big building.

"Of all the men under whom 'Eddie,' as he is universally called, has served he has become most attached to Judge Day, whom he says is the finest man he ever saw.

"Minister Polo was determined not to receive the ultimatum. He was confident he would receive a private tip from the White House, which would enable him to demand his passports before the ultimatum was served upon him. Then he could refuse to receive it, saying that he was no longer Minister. It will be remembered that

Spain handed Minister Woodford his passports before the American representative could present the ultimatum to the Spanish Government.

"Judge Day's training as a country lawyer stood him in good stead. He had learned the value of being the first to get in an attachment.

"The ultimatum was placed in a large, square envelope, that might have contained an invitation to dinner. It was natural that it should be given to 'Eddie' Savoy. He had gained the sobriquet of the nation's 'bouncer,' from the fact that he had handed Lord Sackville-West and Minister De Lome their passports.

"It was 11:30 o'clock on Wednesday morning when 'Eddie' Savoy pushed the electric button at the front door of the Spanish Legation, in Massachusetts avenue. The old Spanish soldier who acted as doorkeeper responded.

" 'Have something here for the Minister,' said Eddie.

"The porter looked at him suspiciously, but he permitted the messenger to pass into the vestibule, which is perhaps six feet square. Beyond the vestibule is a passage that leads to the large central hall. The Minister stood in the hall. In one hand he held an envelope. It was addressed to the Secretary of State. It contained a request for the passports of the Minister and his suite. Senor Polo had personally brought the document from the chancellory above.

"When the porter presented the letter just

Eddie Savoy.

brought by the Department of State's messenger, Senor Polo grasped it in his quick, nervous way. He opened the envelope and realized instantly that he had been outwitted. A cynical smile passed over the Minister's face as he handed his request for passports to 'Eddie,' who bowed and smiled on the Minister.

"Senor Polo stepped back into the hall and started to read the ultimatum carefully. But he stopped and turned his head toward the door.

" 'This is indeed Jeffersonian simplicity,' he said.

" 'Eddie' Savoy felt very badly over the incident, because he had learned to like Minister Polo personally.

" 'He was so pleasant that I felt like asking him to stay a little longer,' said 'Eddie,' 'but I didn't, for that wouldn't have been diplomatic. When you have been in this department twenty-five or thirty years you learn never to say what you want to say and never to speak unless you think twice.'

"Wherefore it will be seen that 'Eddie' Savoy has mastered the first principles of diplomacy."— "N. Y. World."

A Copy of the Resolution by Congress was also cabled to Minister Woodford, at Madrid, to be officially transmitted to the Spanish Government, fixing the 23d as the limit for its reply, but the Spanish Minister of Foreign Affairs had already learned of the action of Congress, and did not

Jose Maceo.

permit Minister Woodford to ask for his passports, but sent them to him on the evening of the 21st, and this was the formal beginning of the war.

A Fatal Step was this for Spain, who evidently, as her newspapers declared, did not think the "American pigs" would fight. She was unaware of the temper of the people, who seemed to those who knew the facts actually thirsting for Spanish blood—a feeling due more or less to thirty years of peace, in which the nation had become restless, and to the fact also that America had some new boats, fine specimens of workmanship, which had been at target practice for a long time and now yearned for the reality, like the boy who has a gun and wants to try it on the real game. The proof of the superiority of American gunnery was demonstrated in every naval battle. The accurate aim of Dewey's gunners at Manilla, and Sampson and Schley's at Santiago, was nothing less than wonderful. No less wonderful, however, was the accuracy of the Americans than the inaccuracy of the Spaniards, who seemed almost unable to hit anything.

While Accrediting the American Navy with its full share of praise for its wonderful accomplishments, let us remember that there is scarcely a boat in the navy flying the American flag but what has a number of "colored sailors" on it, who, along with others, help to make up its greatness and superiority.

CHAPTER II.

THE BEGINNING OF HOSTILITIES.

A COLORED HERO IN THE NAVY.

History records the Negro as the first man to fall in three wars of America—Crispus Attucks in the Boston massacre, March 5, 1770; an unknown Negro in Baltimore when the Federal troops were mobbed in that city en route to the front, and Elijah B. Tunnell, of Accomac County, Virginia, who fell simultaneously with or a second before Ensign Bagley, of the torpedo boat Winslow, in the harbor of Cardenas, May 11, 1898, in the Spanish-American war.

Elijah B. Tunnell was employed as cabin cook on the Winslow. The boat, under a severe fire from masked batteries of the Spanish on shore, was disabled. The Wilmington came to her rescue, the enemy meanwhile still pouring on a heavy fire. It was difficult to get the "line" fastened so that the Winslow could be towed off out of range of the Spanish guns. Realizing the danger the boat and crew were in, and anxious to be of service, Tunnell left his regular work and went on deck to assist in "making fast" the two boats, and while thus engaged a shell came, which, bursting over the group of workers, killed him and three others. It has been stated in newspaper reports of this incident that it was an ill-aimed shell of one of the American boats that killed Tunnell and Bagley. Tunnell was taken on board the Wilmington with both legs blown off, and fearfully mutilated. Turning to those about him he asked, "Did we win in the fight, boys?" The reply was, "Yes." He said, "Then I die happy." While others fell at the post of duty it may be said of this brave Negro that he fell while doing "more" than his duty. He might have kept out of harm's way if he had desired, but seeing the situation he rushed forward to relieve it as best he could, and died a "volunteer" in service, doing what others ought to have done. All honor to the memory of Elijah B. Tunnell, who fell, if not the first, certainly simultaneous with the first martyr of the Spanish-American war. While our white fellow-citizens justly herald the fame of Ensign Bagley, who was known to the author from his youth, let our colored patriots proclaim the heroism of Tunnell of Accomac. While not ranking as an official in the navy, yet he was brave, he was faithful and we may inscribe over his grave that "he died doing what he could for his country."

War between the United States and Spain began April 21, 1898. Actual hostilities ended August 12, 1898, by the signing of the protocol by the Secretary of State of the United States for the United States and M. Cambon, the French Ambassador at Washington, acting for Spain.

The war lasted 114 days. The Americans were victorious in every regular engagement. In the three days' battle around Santiago, the Americans lost 22 officers and 208 men killed, and 81 officers and 1,203 men wounded, and 79 missing. The Spanish loss as best estimated was near 1,600 officers and men killed and wounded.

Santiago was surrendered July 17, 1898, with something over 22,000 troops.

General Shafter estimates in his report the American forces as numbering 16,072 with 815 officers.

CHAPTER III.

SERGEANT - MAJOR PULLEN OF THE 25TH INFANTRY DESCRIBES THE CONDUCT OF THE NEGRO SOL-DIERS AROUND EL CANEY.

THE TWENTY-FIFTH U. S. INFANTRY—ITS STATION BEFORE THE SPANISH-AMERICAN WAR AND TRIP TO TAMPA, FLORIDA —THE PART IT TOOK IN THE FIGHT AT EL CANEY.

When our magnificent battleship Maine was sunk in Havana harbor, February 15, 1898, the 25th U. S. Infantry was scattered in western Montana, doing garrison duty, with headquarters at Fort Missoula. This regiment had been stationed in the West since 1880, when it came up from Texas where it had been from its consolidation in 1869, fighting Indians, building roads, etc., for the pioneers of that State and New Mexico. In consequence of the regiment's constant frontier service, very little was known of it outside of army circles. As a matter of course it was known that it was a colored regiment, but its praises had never been sung.

Strange to say, although the record of this regiment was equal to any in the service, it had always occupied remote stations, except a short period, from about May, 1880, to about August, 1885, when headquarters, band and a few com-

Sergeant Frank W. Pullen,
Who was in the Charge on El Caney, as a member of the Twenty-fifth U. S. Infantry.

panies were stationed at Fort Snelling, near St. Paul, Minnesota.

Since the days of reconstruction, when a great part of the country (the South especially) saw the regular soldier in a low state of discipline, and when the possession of a sound physique was the only requirement necessary for the recruit to enter the service of the United States, people in general had formed an opinion that the regular soldier, generally, and the Negro soldier in particular, was a most undesirable element to have in a community. Therefore, the Secretary of War, in ordering changes in stations of troops from time to time (as is customary to change troops from severe climates to mild ones and vice versa, that equal justice might be done all), had repeatedly overlooked the 25th Infantry; or had only ordered it from Minnesota to the Dakotas and Montana, in the same military department, and in a climate more severe for troops to serve in than any in the United States. This gallant regiment of colored soldiers served eighteen years in that climate, where, in winter, which lasts five months or more, the temperature falls as low as 55 degrees below zero, and in summer rises to over 100 degrees in the shade and where mosquitos rival the Jersey breed.

Before Congress had reached a conclusion as to what should be done in the Maine disaster, an order had been issued at headquarters of the army directing the removal of the regiment to

the department of the South, one of the then recently organized departments.

At the time when the press of the country was
urging a declaration of war, and when Minister
Woodford, at Madrid, was exhausting all the
arts of peace, in order that the United States
might get prepared for war, the men of the 25th
Infantry were sitting around red-hot stoves, in
their comfortable quarters in Montana, discuss-
ing the doings of Congress, impatient for a
move against Spain. After great excitement and
what we looked upon as a long delay, a tel-
egraphic order came. Not for us to leave for the
Department of the South, but to go to that lonely
sun-parched sandy island Dry Tortugas. In the
face of the fact that the order was for us to go to
that isolated spot, where rebel prisoners were
carried and turned loose during the war of the
rebellion, being left there without guard, there
being absolutely no means of escape, and where
it would have been necessary for our safety to
have kept Sampson's fleet in sight, the men received the news with gladness and cheered as the
order was read to them. The destination was
changed to Key West, Florida, then to Chickamauga Park, Georgia. It seemed that the War
Department did not know what to do with the
soldiers at first.

Early Sunday morning, April 10, 1898, Easter
Sunday, amidst tears of lovers and others en-
deared by long acquaintance and kindness, and

the enthusiastic cheers of friends and well-wishers, the start was made for Cuba.

It is a fact worthy of note that Easter services in all the churches in Missoula, Montana, a town of over ten thousand inhabitants, was postponed the morning of the departure of the 25th Infantry, and the whole town turned out to bid us farewell. Never before were soldiers more encouraged to go to war than we. Being the first regiment to move, from the West, the papers had informed the people of our route. At every station there was a throng of people who cheered as we passed. Everywhere the Stars and Stripes could be seen. Everybody had caught the war fever. We arrived at Chickamauga Park about April 15, 1898, being the first regiment to arrive at that place. We were a curiosity. Thousands of people, both white and colored, from Chattanooga, Tenn., visited us daily. Many of them had never seen a colored soldier. The behavior of the men was such that even the most prejudiced could find no fault. We underwent a short period of acclimation at this place, then moved on to Tampa, Fla., where we spent a month more of acclimation. All along the route from Missoula, Montana, with the exception of one or two places in Georgia, we had been received most cordially. But in Georgia, outside of the Park, it mattered not if we were soldiers of the United States, and going to fight for the honor of our country and the freedom of an oppressed and starving people, we were "niggers," as they called us, and treated us with contempt. There was no enthusiasm nor Stars and Stripes in Georgia. That is the kind of "united country" we saw in the South. I must pass over the events and incidents of camp life at Chickamauga and Tampa. Up to this time our trip had seemed more like a Sunday-school excursion than anything else. But when, on June 6th, we were ordered to divest ourselves of all clothing and equipage, except such as was necessary to campaigning in a tropical climate, for the first time the ghost of real warfare arose before us.

ON BOARD THE TRANSPORT.

The regiment went aboard the Government transport No. 14—Concho—June 7, 1898. On the same vessel were the 14th U. S. Infantry, a battalion of the 2d Massachusetts Volunteers and Brigade Headquarters, aggregating about 1,300 soldiers, exclusive of the officers. This was the beginning of real hardship. The transport had either been a common freighter or a cattle ship. Whatever had been its employment before being converted into a transport, I am sure of one thing, it was neither fit for man nor beast when soldiers were transported in it to Cuba. The actual carrying capacity of the vessel as a transport was, in my opinion, about 900 soldiers, exclusive of the officers, who, as a rule, surround themselves with every possible comfort, even in actual warfare. A good many times, as on this occasion, the desire and demand of the officers for comfort worked serious hardships for the enlisted men. The lower decks had been filled with bunks. Alas! the very thought of those things of torture makes me shudder even now. They were arranged in rows, lengthwise the ship, of course, with aisles only two feet wide between each row. The dimensions of a man's bunk was 6 feet long, 2 feet wide and 2 feet high, and they were arranged in tiers of four, with a four-inch board on either side to keep one from rolling out. The Government had furnished no bedding at all. Our bedding consisted of one blanket as mattress and haversack for pillow. The 25th Infantry was assigned to the lower deck, where there was no light, except the small portholes when the gangplank was closed. So dark was it that candles were burned all day. There was no air except what came down the canvas air-shafts when they were turned to the breeze. The heat of that place was almost unendurable. Still our Brigade Commander issued orders that no one would be allowed to sleep on the main deck. That order was the only one to my knowledge during the whole campaign that was not obeyed by the colored soldiers. It is an unreported fact that a portion of the deck upon which the 25th Infantry took passage to Cuba was flooded during the entire journey.

Before leaving Port Tampa the Chief Surgeon

of the expedition came aboard and made an inspection, the result of which was the taking off of the ship the volunteer battalion, leaving still on board about a thousand men. Another noteworthy fact is that for seven days the boat was tied to the wharf at Port Tampa, and we were not allowed to go ashore, unless an officer would take a whole company off to bathe and exercise. This was done, too, in plain sight of other vessels, the commander of which gave their men the privilege of going ashore at will for any purpose whatever. It is very easy to imagine the hardship that was imposed upon us by withholding the privilege of going ashore, when it is understood that there were no seats on the vessel for a poor soldier. On the main deck there were a large number of seats, but they were all reserved for the officers. A sentinel was posted on either side of the ship near the middle hatchway, and no soldier was allowed to go abaft for any purpose, except to report to his superior officer or on some other official duty.

Finally the 14th of June came. While bells were ringing, whistles blowing and bands playing cheering strains of music, the transports formed "in fleet in column of twos," and under convoy of some of the best war crafts of our navy, and while the thousands on shore waved us godspeed, moved slowly down the bay on its mission to avenge the death of the heroes of our gallant Maine and to free suffering Cuba.

The transports were scarcely out of sight of land when an order was issued by our Brigade Commander directing that the two regiments on board should not intermingle, and actually drawing the "color line" by assigning the white regiment to the port and the 25th Infantry to the starboard side of the vessel. The men of the two regiments were on the best of terms, both having served together during mining troubles in Montana. Still greater was the surprise of everyone when another order was issued from the same source, directing that the white regiment should make coffee first, all the time, and detailing a guard to see that the order was carried out. All of these things were done seemingly to humiliate us and without a word of protest from our officers. We suffered without complaint. God only knows how it was we lived through those fourteen days on that miserable vessel. We lived through those days and were fortunate enough not to have a burial at sea.

OPERATIONS AGAINST SANTIAGO.

We landed in Cuba June 22, 1898. Our past hardships were soon forgotten. It was enough to stir the heart of any lover of liberty to witness that portion of Gomez's ragged army, under command of General Castillo, lined up to welcome us to their beautiful island, and to guide and guard our way to the Spanish strongholds. To call it a ragged army is by no means a misnomer. The greater portion of those poor fellows were both coatless and shoeless, many of them being almost nude. They were by no means careful about their uniform. The thing every one seemed careful about was his munitions of war, for each man had his gun, ammunition and machete. Be it remembered that this portion of the Cuban army was almost entirely composed of black Cubans.

After landing we halted long enough to ascertain that all the men of the regiment were "present or accounted for," then marched into the jungle of Cuba, following an old unused trail. General Shafter's orders were to push forward without delay. And the 25th Infantry has the honor of leading the march from the landing at Baiquiri or Daiquiri (both names being used in official reports) the first day the army of invasion entered the island. I do not believe any newspaper has ever published this fact.

There was no time to be lost, and the advance of the American army of invasion in the direction of Santiago, the objective point, was rapid. Each day, as one regiment would halt for a rest or reach a suitable camping ground, another would pass. In this manner several regiments had succeeded in passing the 25th Infantry by the morning of June 24th. At that time the 1st Volunteer Cavalry (Rough Riders) was leading the march.

THE FIRST BATTLE.

On the morning of June 24th the Rough Riders struck camp early, and was marching along the trail at a rapid gait, at "route step," in any order suitable to the size of the road. Having marched several miles through a well-wooded country, they came to an opening near where the road forked. They turned into the left fork; at that moment, without the least warning, the Cubans leading the march having passed on unmolested, a volley from the Spanish behind a stone fort on top of the hill on both sides of the road was fired into their ranks. They were at first disconcerted, but rallied at once and began firing in the direction from whence came the volleys. They could not advance, and dared not retreat, having been caught in a sunken place in the road, with a barbed-wire fence on one side and a precipitous hill on the other. They held their ground, but could do no more. The Spanish poured volley after volley into their ranks. At the moment when it looked as if the whole regiment would be swept down by the steel-jacketed bullets from the Mausers, four troops of the 10th U. S. Cavalry (colored) came up on "double time." Little thought the Spaniards that these "smoked Yankees" were so formidable. Perhaps they thought to stop those black boys by their relentless fire, but those boys knew no stop. They halted for a second, and having with them a Hotchkiss gun, soon knocked down the Spanish

Corporal Brown,

Who was killed at a Hotchkiss gun while shelling the Spanish blockhouse to save the Rough Riders.

improvised fort, cut the barb-wire, making an opening for the Rough Riders, started the charge, and, with the Rough Riders, routed the Spaniards, causing them to retreat in disorder, leaving their dead and some wounded behind. The Spaniards made a stubborn resistance. So hot was their fire directed at the men at the Hotchkiss gun that a head could not be raised, and men crawled on their stomachs like snakes loading and firing. It is an admitted fact that the Rough Riders could not have dislodged the Spanish by themselves without great loss, if at all.

The names of Captain A. M. Capron, Jr., and Sergeant Hamilton Fish, Jr., of the Rough Riders, who were killed in this battle, have been immortalized, while that of Corporal Brown, 10th Cavalry, who manned the Hotchkiss gun in this fight, without which the American loss in killed and wounded would no doubt have been counted by hundreds, and who was killed by the side of his gun, is unknown by the public.

At the time the battle of the Rough Riders was fought the 25th Infantry was within hearing distance of the battle and received orders to reinforce them, which they could have done in less than two hours, but our Brigade Commander in marching to the scene of battle took the wrong trail, seemingly on purpose, and when we arrived at the place of battle twilight was fading into darkness.

The march in the direction of Santiago continued, until the evening of June 30th found us bivouacked in the road less than two miles from El Caney. At the first glimpse of day on the first day of July word was passed along the line for the companies to "fall in." No bugle call was sounded, no coffee was made, no noise allowed. We were nearing the enemy, and every effort was made to surprise him. We had been told that El Caney was well fortified, and so we found it.

The first warning the people had of a foe being near was the roar of our field artillery and the bursting of a shell in their midst. The battle was on. In many cases an invading army serves notice of a bombardment, but in this case it was incompatible with military strategy. Non-combatants, women and children, all suffered, for to have warned them so they might have escaped would also have given warning to the Spanish forces of our approach. The battle opened at dawn and lasted until dark. When our troops reached the point from which they were to make the attack, the Spanish lines of entrenched soldiers could not be seen. The only thing indicating their position was the blockhouse situated on the highest point of a very steep hill. The undergrowth was so dense that one could not see, on a line, more than fifty yards ahead. The Spaniards, from their advantageous position in the blockhouse and trenches on the hill top, had located the American forces in the bushes and opened a fusilade upon them. The Americans replied with great vigor, being ordered to fire at the blockhouse and to the right and left of it, steadily advancing as they fired. All of the regiments engaged in the battle of El Caney had not reached their positions when the battle was precipitated by the artillery firing on the blockhouse. The 25th Infantry was among that number. In marching to its position some companies of the 2d Massachusetts Volunteers were met retreating; they were completely whipped, and took occasion to warn us, saying: "Boys, there is no use to go up there, you cannot see a thing; they are slaughtering our men!" Such news made us feel "shaky," not having, at the time, been initiated. We marched up, however, in order and were under fire for nine hours. Many barbed-wire obstructions were encountered, but the men never faltered. Finally, late in the afternoon, our brave Lieutenant Kinnison said to another officer: "We cannot take the trenches without charging them." Just as he was about to give the order for the bugler to sound "the charge" he was wounded and carried to the rear. The men were then fighting like demons. Without a word of command, though led by that gallant and intrepid Second Lieutenant J. A. Moss, 25th Infantry, some one gave a yell and the 25th Infantry was off, alone, to the charge. The 4th

U. S. Infantry, fighting on the left, halted when those dusky heroes made the dash with a yell which would have done credit to a Comanche Indian. No one knows who started the charge; one thing is certain, at the time it was made excitement was running high; each man was a captain for himself and fighting accordingly. Brigadier Generals, Colonels, Lieutenant-Colonels, Majors, etc., were not needed at the time the 25th Infantry made the charge on El Caney, and those officers simply watched the battle from convenient points, as Lieutenants and enlisted men made the charge alone. It has been reported that the 12th U. S. Infantry made the charge, assisted by the 25th Infantry, but it is a recorded fact that the 25th Infantry fought the battle alone, the 12th Infantry coming up after the firing had nearly ceased. Private T. C. Butler, Company H, 25th Infantry, was the first man to enter the blockhouse at El Caney, and took possession of the Spanish flag for his regiment. An Officer of the 12th Infantry came up while Butler was in the house and ordered him to give up the flag, which he was compelled to do, but not until he had torn a piece off the flag to substantiate his report to his Colonel of the injustice which had been done to him. Thus, by using the authority given him by his shoulder-straps, this officer took for his regiment that which had been won by the hearts' blood of some of the bravest, though black, soldiers of Shafter's army.

The charge of El Caney has been little spoken of, but it was quite as great a show of bravery as the famous taking of San Juan Hill.

A word more in regard to the charge. It was not the glorious run from the edge of some near-by thicket to the top of a small hill, as many may imagine. This particular charge was a tough, hard climb, over sharp, rising ground, which, were a man in perfect physical strength, he would climb slowly. Part of the charge was made over soft, plowed ground, a part through a lot of prickly pineapple plants and barbed-wire entanglements. It was slow, hard work, under a blazing July sun and a perfect hail-storm of bullets, which, thanks to the poor marksmanship of the Spaniards, "went high."

It has been generally admitted, by all fair-minded writers, that the colored soldiers saved the day both at El Caney and San Juan Hill.

Notwithstanding their heroic services, they were still to be subjected, in many cases, to more hardships than their white brother in arms. When the flag of truce was, in the afternoon of July 3d, seen, each man breathed a sigh of relief, for the strain had been very great upon us. During the next eleven days men worked like ants, digging trenches, for they had learned a lesson of fighting in the open field. The work went on night and day. The 25th Infantry worked harder than any other regiment, for as soon as they would finish a trench they were ordered to

Charge on El Caney—Twenty-fifth Infantry.

move; in this manner they were kept moving and digging new trenches for eleven days. The trenches left were each time occupied by a white regiment.

On July 14th it was decided to make a demonstration in front of Santiago, to draw the fire of the enemy and locate his position. Two companies of colored soldiers (25th Infantry) were selected for this purpose, actually deployed as skirmishers and started in advance. General Shafter, watching the movement from a distant hill, saw that such a movement meant to sacrifice those men, without any or much good resulting, therefore had them recalled. Had the movement been completed it is probable that not a man would have escaped death or serious wounds. When the news came that General Toral had decided to surrender, the 25th Infantry was a thousand yards or more nearer the city of Santiago than any regiment in the army, having entrenched themselves along the railroad leading into the city.

The following enlisted men of the 25th Infantry were commissioned for their bravery at El Caney: First Sergeant Andrew J. Smith, First Sergeant Macon Russell, First Sergeant Wyatt Huffman and Sergeant Wm. McBryar. Many more were recommended, but failed to receive commissions. It is a strange incident that all the above-named men are native North Carolinians, but First Sergeant Huffman, who is from Tennessee.

The Negro played a most important part in the Spanish-American war. He was the first to move from the West; first at Camp Thomas, Chickamauga Park, Ga., first in the jungle of Cuba; among the first killed in battle; first in the blockhouse at El Caney, and nearest to the enemy when he surrendered.

FRANK W. PULLEN, JR.,

Ex-Sergeant-Major 25th U. S. Infantry.

Enfield, N. C., March 23, 1899.

BUFFALO TROOPERS, THE NAME BY WHICH NEGRO SOLDIERS ARE KNOWN.

THEY COMPRISE SEVERAL OF THE CRACK REGIMENTS IN OUR ARMY—THE INDIANS STAND IN ABJECT TERROR OF THEM—THEIR AWFUL YELLS WON A BATTLE WITH THE REDSKINS.

"It is not necessary to revert to the Civil War to prove that American Negroes are faithful, devoted wearers of uniforms," says a Washington man, who has seen service in both the army and the navy. "There are at the present time four regiments of Negro soldiers in the regular army of the United States—two outfits of cavalry and two of infantry. All four of these regiments have been under fire in important Indian campaigns, and there is yet to be recorded a single

instance of a man in any of the four layouts
showing the white feather, and the two cavalry
regiments of Negroes have, on several occasions,
found themselves in very serious situations.
While the fact is well known out on the frontier,
I don't remember ever having seen it mentioned
back here that an American Indian has a deadly
fear of an American Negro. The most utterly
reckless, dare-devil savage of the copper hue
stands literally in awe of a Negro, and the
blacker the Negro the more the Indian quails.
I can't understand why this should be, for the
Indians decline to give their reasons for fearing
the black men, but the fact remains that even
a very bad Indian will give the mildest-man-
nered Negro imaginable all the room he wants,
and to spare, as any old regular army soldier
who has frontiered will tell you. The Indians,
I fancy, attribute uncanny and eerie qualities
to the blacks.

"The cavalry troop to which I belonged
soldiered alongside a couple of troops of the
9th Cavalry, a black regiment, up in the Sioux
country eight or nine years ago. We were per-
forming chain guard, hemming-in duty, and it
was our chief business to prevent the savages
from straying from the reservation. We
weren't under instructions to riddle them if
they attempted to pass our guard posts, but
were authorized to tickle them up to any rea-
sonable extent, short of maiming them, with our

bayonets, if any of them attempted to bluff past us. Well, the men of my troop had all colors of trouble while on guard in holding the savages in. The Ogalallas would hardly pay any attention to the white sentries of the chain guard, and when they wanted to pass beyond the guard limits they would invariably pick out a spot for passage that was patrolled by a white 'post-humper.' But the guards of the two black troops didn't have a single run-in with the savages. The Indians made it a point to remain strictly away from the Negro soldiers' guard posts. Moreover, the black soldiers got ten times as much obedience from the Indians loafing around the tepees and wickleups as did we of the white outfit. The Indians would fairly jump to obey the uniformed Negroes. I remember seeing a black sergeant make a minor chief go down to a creek to get a pail of water—an unheard-of thing, for the chiefs, and even the ordinary bucks among the Sioux always make their squaws perform this sort of work. This chief was sunning himself, reclining, beside his tepee, when his squaw started with the bucket for the creek some distance away. The Negro sergeant saw the move. He walked up to the lazy, grunting savage.

"'Look a-yeah, yo' spraddle-nosed, yalluh voodoo nigguh,' said the black sergeant—he was as black as a stove-pipe—to the blinking chief, 'jes' shake yo' no-count bones an' tote dat

wattuh yo'se'f. Yo' ain' no bettuh to pack
wattuh dan Ah am, yo' heah me.'

"The heap-much Indian chief didn't understand a word of what the Negro sergeant said
to him, but he understands pantomime all right,
and when the black man in uniform grabbed the
pail out of the squaw's hand and thrust it into
the dirty paw of the chief, the chief went after
that bucket of water, and he went a-loping, too.

"The Sioux will hand down to their children's
children the story of a charge that a couple of
Negro cavalry troops made during the Pine
Ridge troubles. It was on the height of the
fracas, and the bad Indians were regularly lined
up for battle. Those two black troops were ordered to make the initial swoop upon them. You
know the noise one black man can make when he
gets right down to the business of yelling. Well,
these two troops of blacks started their terrific
whoop in unison when they were a mile away
from the waiting Sioux, and they got warmed
up and in better practice with every jump their
horses made. I give you my solemn word that
in the ears of us of the white outfit, stationed
three miles away, the yelps those two Negro
troops of cavalry gave sounded like the carnival
whooping of ten thousand devils. The Sioux
weren't scared a little bit by the approaching
clouds of alkali dust, but, all the same, when the
two black troops were more than a quarter of a
mile away the Indians broke and ran as if the

old boy himself were after them, and it was then an easy matter to round them up and disarm them. The chiefs afterward confessed that they were scared out by the awful howling of the black soldiers.

"Ever since the war the United States navy has had a fair representation of Negro bluejackets, and they make first-class naval tars. There is not a ship in the navy to-day that hasn't from six to a dozen, anyhow, of Negroes on its muster rolls. The Negro sailors' names very rarely get enrolled on the bad conduct lists. They are obedient, sober men and good seamen. There are many petty officers among them."— "The Planet."

THE CHARGE OF THE "NIGGER NINTH" ON SAN JUAN HILL.

BY GEORGE E. POWELL.

Hark! O'er the drowsy trooper's dream,
There comes a martial metal's scream,
    That startles one and all!
It is the word, to wake, to die!
To hear the foeman's fierce defy!
To fling the column's battle-cry!
    The "boots and saddles" call.

The shimmering steel, the glow of morn,
The rally-call of battle-horn,
Proclaim a day of carnage, born
    For better or for ill.
Above the pictured tentage white,
Above the weapons glinting bright,
The day god casts a golden light
    Across the San Juan Hill.

"Forward!" "Forward!" comes the cry,
As stalwart columns, ambling by,
Stride over graves that, waiting, lie
    Undug in mother earth!
Their goal, the flag of fierce Castile
Above her serried ranks of steel,
Insensate to the cannon's peal
    That gives the battle birth!

As brawn as black—a fearless foe;
Grave, grim and grand, they onward go,
    To conquer or to die!
The rule of right; the march of might;
A dusky host from darker night,
Responsive to the morning light,
    To work the martial will!
And o'er the trench and trembling earth,
The morn that gives the battle birth
    Is on the San Juan Hill!

Hark! sounds again the bugle call!
Let ring the rifles over all,
To shriek above the battle-pall
    The war-god's jubilee!
Their's, were bondmen, low, and long;
Their's, once weak against the strong;
Their's, to strike and stay the wrong,
    That strangers might be free!

And on, and on, for weal or woe,
The tawny faces grimmer go,
That bade no mercy to a foe
    That pities but to kill.
"Close up!" "Close up!" is heard, and said,
And yet the rain of steel and lead
Still leaves a livid trail of red
    Upon the San Juan Hill!

"Charge!" "Charge!" The bugle peals again;
'Tis life or death for Roosevelt's men!—
    The Mausers make reply!
Aye! speechless are those swarthy sons,
Save for the clamor of the guns—
    Their only battle-cry!
The lowly stain upon each face,
The taunt still fresh of prouder race,
But speeds the step that springs a-pace,
    To succor or to die!

With rifles hot—to waist-band nude;
The brawn beside the pampered dude;
The cowboy king—one grave—and rude—
    To shelter him who falls!
One breast—and bare,—howe'er begot,
The low, the high—one common lot:
The world's distinction all forgot
    When Freedom's bugle calls!

No faltering step, no fitful start;
None seeking less than all his part;
One watchword springing from each heart,—
    Yet on, and onward still!

Charge on San Juan Hill.

The sullen sound of tramp and tread;
Abe Lincoln's flag still overhead;
They followed where the angels led
    The way, up San Juan Hill!

And where the life stream ebbs and flows,
And stains the track of trenchant blows
    That met no meaner steel,

The bated breath—the battle yell—
The turf in slippery crimson, tell
Where Castile's proudest colors fell
    With wounds that never heal!

Where every trooper found a wreath
Of glory for his sabre sheath;
    And earned the laurels well;
With feet to field and face to foe,
In lines of battle lying low,
    The sable soldiers fell!

And where the black and brawny breast
Gave up its all—life's richest, best,
To find the tomb's eternal rest
    A dream of freedom still!
A groundless creed was swept away,
With brand of "coward"—a time-worn say—
And he blazed the path, a better way
    Up the side of San Juan Hill!
For black or white, on the scroll of fame,
The blood of the hero dyes the same;
    And ever, ever will!

*   *   *   *   *   *   *   *

    Sleep, trooper, sleep; thy sable brow,
    Amid the living laurel now,
        Is wound in wreaths of fame!
    Nor need the graven granite stone,
    To tell of garlands all thine own—
        To hold a soldier's name!

[In the city of New Orleans, in 1866, two thousand two hundred
and sixty-six ex-slaves were recruited for the service. None but
the largest and blackest Negroes were accepted. From these were
formed the Twenty-fourth and Twenty-fifth Infantry, and the
Ninth and Tenth Cavalry. All four are famous fighting regiments,
and the two cavalry commands have earned the proudest distinction.
But the record of the Ninth Cavalry, better known as the "Nigger
Ninth," in its thirty-two years of service in the Indian wars, in
the military history of the border stands without a peer and is.
without exception, the most famous fighting regiment in the United
States service.]

CHAPTER IV.

COLONEL THEODORE B. ROOSEVELT TELLS OF THE BRAVERY OF NEGRO SOLDIERS.

When Colonel Theodore Roosevelt returned from the command of the famous Rough Riders, he delivered a farewell address to his men, in which he made the following kind reference to the gallant Negro soldiers:

"Now, I want to say just a word more to some of the men I see standing around not of your number. I refer to the colored regiments, who occupied the right and left flanks of us at Guasimas, the Ninth and Tenth cavalry regiments. The Spaniards called them 'Smoked Yankees,' but we found them to be an excellent breed of Yankees. I am sure that I speak the sentiments of officers and men in the assemblage when I say that between you and the other cavalry regiments there exists a tie which we trust will never be broken."—"Colored American."

The foregoing compliments to the Negro soldiers by Colonel Roosevelt started up an avalanche of additional praise for them, out of which the fact came, that but for the Ninth and Tenth Cavalry (colored) coming up at Las Guasimas,

Colonel Theodore B. Roosevelt.

destroying the Spanish blockhouse and driving
the Spaniards off, when Roosevelt and his men
had been caught in a trap, with a barbed-wire
fence on one side and a precipice on the other,
not only the brave Capron and Fish, but the
whole of his command would have been annihi-
lated by the Spanish sharpshooters, who were
firing with smokeless powder under cover, and
picking off the Rough Riders one by one, who
could not see the Spaniards. To break the force
of this unfavorable comment on the Rough
Riders, it is claimed that Colonel Roosevelt
made the following criticism of the colored soldiers in general and of a few of them in particular, in an article written by him for the April
"Scribner"; and a letter replying to the
Colonel's strictures follows by Sergeant Holliday, who was an "eyewitness" to the incident:

Colonel Roosevelt's criticism was, in substance, that colored soldiers were of no avail
without white officers; that when the white
commissioned officers are killed or disabled, colored non-commissioned officers could not be
depended upon to keep up a charge already
begun; that about a score of colored infantry-
men, who had drifted into his command, weakened on the hill at San Juan under the galling
Spanish fire, and started to the rear, stating
that they intended finding their regiments or
to assist the wounded; whereupon he drew his
revolver and ordered them to return to ranks

and there remain, and that he would shoot the first man who didn't obey him; and that after that he had no further trouble.

Colonel Roosevelt is sufficiently answered in the following letter of Sergeant Holliday, and the point especially made by many eyewitnesses (white) who were engaged in that fight is, as related in Chapter Five of this book, that the Negro troops made the charges both at San Juan and El Caney after nearly all their officers had been killed or wounded. Upon what facts, therefore, does Colonel Roosevelt base his conclusions that Negro soldiers will not fight without commissioned officers, when the only real test of this question happened around Santiago and showed just the contrary of what he states? We prefer to take the results at El Caney and San Juan as against Colonel Roosevelt's imagination.

COLONEL ROOSEVELT'S ERROR.

TRUE STORY OF THE INCIDENT HE MAGNIFIED TO OUR HURT— THE WHITE OFFICERS' HUMBUG SKINNED OF ITS HIDE BY SERGEANT HOLLIDAY—UNWRITTEN HISTORY.

To the Editor of the "New York Age":

Having read in "The Age" of April 13th an editorial entitled "Our Troops in Cuba," which brings to my notice for the first time a statement made by Colonel Roosevelt, which, though in some parts true, if read by those who do not know the exact facts and circumstances surrounding the case, will certainly give rise to the wrong impression of colored men as soldiers, and hurt them for many a day to come, and as I was an eyewitness to the most important incidents mentioned in that statement, I deem it a duty I owe, not only to the fathers, mothers, sisters and brothers of those soldiers, and to the soldiers themselves, but to their posterity and the race in general, to be always ready to make an unprejudiced refutation of such charges, and to do all in my power to place the colored soldier where he properly belongs—among the bravest and most trustworthy of this land.

In the beginning, I wish to say that from what I saw of Colonel Roosevelt in Cuba, and the impression his frank countenance made upon me, I cannot believe that he made that statement maliciously. I believe the Colonel thought he spoke the exact truth. But did he know, that of the four officers connected with two certain troops of the Tenth Cavalry one was killed and three were so seriously wounded as to cause them to be carried from the field, and the command of these two troops fell to the first sergeants, who led them triumphantly to the front? Does he know that both at Las Guasima and San Juan Hill the greater part of Troop B, of the Tenth Cavalry, was separated from its commanding officer by accidents of battle and was led to the front by its first sergeant?

When we reached the enemy's works on San Juan Hill our organizations were very badly mixed, few company commanders having their whole companies or none of somebody else's company. As it was, Capt. Watson, my troop commander, reached the crest of the hill with about eight or ten men of his troop, all the rest having been accidentally separated from him by the thick underbrush during the advance, and being at that time, as was subsequently shown, on the firing line under some one else pushing to the front. We kept up the forward movement, and finally halted on the heights overlooking Santiago, where Colonel Roosevelt, with a very thin line, had preceded us and was holding the hill. Here Captain Watson told us to remain while he went to another part of the line to look for the rest of his troop. He did not come to that part of the field again.

The Colonel made a slight error when he said his mixed command contained some colored infantry. All the colored troops in that command were cavalrymen. His command consisted mostly of Rough Riders, with an aggregate of about one troop of the Tenth Cavalry, a few of the Ninth and a few of the First Regular Cavalry, with a half dozen officers. Every few minutes brought men from the rear, everybody seeming to be anxious to get to the firing line. For a while we kept up a desultory fire, but as we could not locate the enemy (he all the time keeping up a hot fire on our position), we became disgusted, and lay down and kept silent. Private Marshall was here seriously wounded while standing in plain view of the enemy, trying to point them out to his comrades.

There were frequent calls for men to carry the wounded to the rear, to go for ammunition, and as night came on, to go for rations and entrenching tools. A few colored soldiers volunteered, as did some from the Rough Riders. It then happened that two men of the Tenth were ordered to the rear by Lieutenant Fleming, Tenth Cavalry, who was then present with part of his troop, for the purpose of bringing either rations or entrenching tools, and Colonel Roosevelt, seeing so many men going to the rear, shouted to them to come back, jumped up and drew his revolver, and told the men of the Tenth that he would shoot the first man who attempted to shirk duty by going to the rear, that he had orders to hold that line and he would do so if he had to shoot every man there to do it. His own men immediately informed him that "you won't have to shoot those men, Colonel. We know those boys." He was also assured by Lieutenant Fleming, of the Tenth, that he would have no trouble keeping them there, and some of our men shouted, in which I joined, that "we will stay with you, Colonel." Everyone who saw the incident knew the Colonel was mistaken about our men trying to shirk duty, but well knew that he could not admit of any heavy detail from his command, so no one thought ill of the matter. Inasmuch as the Colonel came to the line of the Tenth the next day and told the men of his threat to shoot some of their members, and, as he expressed it, he had seen his mistake and found them to be far different men from what he supposed. I thought he was sufficiently conscious of his error not to make so ungrateful a statement about us at a time when the Nation is about to forget our past service.

Had the Colonel desired to note the fact, he would have seen that when orders came the next day to relieve the detachment of the Tenth from that part of the field, he commanded just as many colored men at that time as he commanded at any other time during the twenty-four hours we were under his command, although colored as well as white soldiers were going and coming all day, and they knew perfectly well where the Tenth Cavalry was posted, and that it was on a line about four hundred yards further from the enemy than Colonel Roosevelt's line. Still, when they obtained permission to go to the rear, they

almost invariably came back to the same position.   Two men of my troop were wounded
while going to the rear for water and taken to
the hospital, and, of course, could not come back.

Our men always made it a rule to join the
nearest command when separated from our
own, and those who had been so unfortunate
as to lose their way altogether were, both colored and white, straggling up from the time
the line was established until far into the
night, showing their determination to reach
the front.

In explaining the desire of our men in going
back to look for their comrades, it should be
stated that, from the contour of the ground,
the Rough Riders were so much in advance of
the Tenth Cavalry that, to reach the latter
regiment from the former, one had really to
go straight to the rear and then turn sharply
to the right; and further, it is a well-known
fact, that in this country most persons of color
feel out of place when they are by force compelled to mingle with white persons, especially
strangers, and although we knew we were doing our duty, and would be treated well as long
as we stood to the front and fought, unfortunately some of our men (and these were all
recruits with less than six months' service) felt
so much out of place that when the firing
lulled they often showed their desire to be with
their commands.   None of our older men did

this. We knew perfectly well that we could give as much assistance there as anywhere else, and that it was our duty to remain until relieved. And we did. White soldiers do not, as a rule, share this feeling with colored soldiers. The fact that a white man knows how well he can make a place for himself among colored people need not be discussed here.

I remember an incident of a recruit of my troop, with less than two months' service, who had come up to our position during the evening of the 1st, having been separated from the troop during the attack on San Juan Hill. The next morning, before the firing began, having seen an officer of the Tenth, who had been sent to Colonel Roosevelt with a message, returning to the regiment, he signified his intention of going back with him, saying he could thus find the regiment. I remonstrated with him without avail, and was only able to keep him from going by informing him of the Colonel's threat of the day before. There was no desire on the part of this soldier to shirk duty. He simply didn't know that he should not leave any part of the firing line without orders. Later, while lying in reserve behind the firing line, I had to use as much persuasion to keep him from firing over the heads of his enemies as I had to keep him with us. He remained with us until he was shot in the shoulder and had to be sent to the rear.

I could give many other incidents of our men's devotion to duty, of their determination to stay until the death, but what's the use? Colonel Roosevelt has said they shirked, and the reading public will take the Colonel at his word and go on thinking they shirked. His statement was uncalled for and uncharitable, and considering the moral and physical effect the advance of the Tenth Cavalry had in weakening the forces opposed to the Colonel's regiment, both at La Guasima and San Juan Hill, altogether ungrateful, and has done us an immeasurable lot of harm.

And further, as to lack of qualifications for command, I will say that when our soldiers, who can and will write history, sever their connections with the Regular Army, and thus release themselves from their voluntary status of military lockjaw, ·and tell what they saw, those who now preach that the Negro is not fit to exercise command over troops, and will go no further than he is led by white officers, will see in print held up for public gaze, much to their chagrin, tales of those Cuban battles that have never been told outside the tent and barrack room, tales that it will not be agreeable for some of them to hear. The public will then learn that not every troop or company of colored soldiers who took part in the assaults on San Juan Hill or El Caney was led or urged forward by its white officer.

It is unfortunate that we had no colored officers in that campaign, and `this thing of white officers for colored troops is exasperating, and I join with "The Age" in saying our motto for the future must be: "No officers, no soldiers."

PRESLEY HOLLIDAY,
Sergeant Troop B, Tenth Cavalry.

Fort Ringgold, Texas, April 22, 1899.

Jacob A. Riis, in "The Outlook," gives the following interesting reading concerning the colored troopers in an article entitled "Roosevelt and His Men":

"It was one of the unexpected things in this campaign that seems destined to set so many things right that out of it should come the appreciation of the colored soldier as man and brother by those even who so lately fought to keep him a chattel. It fell to the lot of General 'Joe' Wheeler, the old Confederate warrior, to command the two regiments of colored troops, the Ninth and Tenth Cavalry, and no one will bear readier testimony than he to the splendid record they made. Of their patience under the manifold hardships of roughing it in the tropics, their helpfulness in the camp and their prowess in battle, their uncomplaining suffering when lying wounded and helpless. Stories enough are told to win for them fairly the real brotherhood with their white-skinned fellows which they crave. The most touching of the many I heard was that of a Negro trooper, who, struck by a bullet that cut an artery in his neck, was lying helpless, in danger of bleeding to death, when a Rough Rider came to his assistance. There was only one thing to be done—to stop the bleeding till a surgeon came. A tourniquet could not be applied where the wound was. The Rough Rider put his thumb on the artery and held it there while he waited. The fighting drifted away over the hill. He followed his comrades with longing eyes till the last was lost to sight. His place was there, but if he abandoned the wounded cavalryman it was to let him die. He dropped his gun and stayed. Not until the battle was won did the surgeon come that way, but the trooper's life was saved. He told of it in the hospital with tears in his voice: 'He done that to me, he did; stayed by me an hour and a half, and me only a nigger.' "

GENERAL NELSON A. MILES PAYS A TRIBUTE TO THE NEGRO SOLDIERS.

Major-General Nelson A. Miles, Commander-in-Chief of the Army of the United States, spoke at the Peace Jubilee at Chicago, October 11th, and said:

"While the chivalry of the South and the yeomanry of the North vied with their devo-

General Nelson A. Miles.

tion to the cause of their country and in their pride in its flag which floated over all, it's a glorious fact that patriotism was not confined to any one section or race for the sacrifice, bravery and fortitude. The white race was accompanied by the gallantry of the black as they swept over intrenched lines and later volunteered to succor the sick, nurse the dying and bury the dead, in the hospitals and the Cuban camps."

This was grandly spoken, and we feel gratified at this recognition of the valor of one of the best races of people the world has ever seen.

"We are coming, boys; it's a little slow and tiresome, but we are coming."—"Colored American."

WITHOUT A PARALLEL.

At a social reunion of the Medal of Honor Legion held for the purpose of welcoming home two of their members, General Nelson A. Miles, commanding the Army of the United States, and Colonel M. Emmett Urell, of the First District Columbia Volunteers, in the course of his remarks General Miles paid the finest possible tribute to the splendid heroism and soldierly qualities evidenced by the men of the Ninth and Tenth Cavalry, and 24th and 25th United States Infantry in the late Santiago campaign, which he epitomized as "without a parallel in the history of the world."

At the close of his remarks, Major C. A. Fleetwood, the only representative of the race present, in behalf of the race extended their heartfelt and warmest thanks for such a magnificent tribute from such a magnificent soldier and man.—"Colored American."

CLEVELAND MOFFITT, IN "LESLIE'S WEEKLY," DESCRIBES THE HEROISM OF A "BLACK COLOR-BEARER."

"Having praised our war leaders sufficiently, in some cases more than sufficiently (witness Hobson), let us give honor to some of the humbler ones, who fought obscurely, but did fine things nevertheless.

"There was Sergeant Berry, for instance, of the Tenth Cavalry, who might have boasted his meed of kisses, too, had he been a white man. At any rate, he rescued the colors of a white regiment from unseemly trampling and bore them safely through the bullets to the top of San Juan Hill. Now, every one knows that the standard of a troop is guarded like a man's own soul, or should be, and how it came that this Third Cavalry banner was lying on the ground that day is something that may never be rightly known. Some white man had left it there, many white men had let it stay there, but Berry, a black man, saw it fluttering in shame and paused in his running long enough to catch it up and lift it high overhead beside his own banner—for he was a color-bearer of the Tenth.

Sergeant Berry,
The first soldier who reached the Blockhouse
on San Juan Hill and hoisted the American flag
in a hail of Spanish bullets.

"Then, with two flags flying above him, and two heavy staves to bear, this powerful Negro (he is literally a giant in strength and stature) charged the heights, while white men and black men cheered him as they pressed behind. Who shall say what temporary demoralization there may have been in this troop of the Third at that critical moment, or what fresh courage may have been fired in them by that black man's act! They say Berry yelled like a demon as he rushed against the Spaniards, and I, for one, am willing to believe that his battle-cry brought fighting energy to his own side as well as terror to the enemy.

"After the fight one of the officers of the Third Cavalry sought Berry out and asked him to give back the trophy fairly won by him, and his to keep, according to the usages of war. And the big Negro handed back the banner with a smile and light word. He had saved the colors and rallied the troop, but it didn't matter much. They could have the flag if they wanted it.

"There are some hundreds of little things like this that we might as well bear in mind, we white men, the next time we start out to decry the Negro!"

PRESIDENT McKINLEY RECOGNIZES THE WORTH OF NEGRO SOLDIERS BY PROMOTION.

PROMOTIONS FOR COLORED SOLDIERS.

Washington, July 30.—Six colored non-commissioned officers who rendered particularly gallant service in the actions around Santiago on July 1st and 2d have been appointed second lieutenants in the two colored immune regiments recently organized under special act of Congress. These men are Sergeants William

General Thomas J. Morgan, LL.D.,
Who says Negroes are Competent to be Officers in the Army.

Washington, Troop F, and John C. Proctor, Troop I, of the 9th Cavalry, and Sergeants William McBryar, Company H; Wyatt Hoffman, Company G; Macon Russell, Company H, and Andrew J. Smith, Company B, of the 25th

Infantry, commanded by Colonel Daggett. Jacob C. Smith, Sergeant Pendergrass, Lieutenant Ray, Sergeant Horace W. Bivins, Lieutenant E. L. Baker, Lieutenant J. H. Hill, Lieutenant Buck.—"N. Y. World."

These promotions were made into the volunteer regiments, which were mustered out after the war, thus leaving the men promoted in the same rank they were before promotion if they chose to reenlist in the regular army. They got no permanent advancement by this act of the President, but the future may develop better things for them.

COMPETENT TO BE OFFICERS—THE VERDICT OF GENERAL THOMAS J. MORGAN, AFTER A STUDY OF THE NEGRO'S QUALITY AS A SOLDIER.

COLOR LINE IN THE ARMY—DIFFICULTY IN MAKING AFRO-AMERICANS COMMISSIONED OFFICERS—HEROISM ON THE FIELD SURE TO REAP REWARD—MORGAN PREFERS NEGRO TROOPS TO THE WHITES.

General Thomas J. Morgan belongs to that class of Caucasian observers who are able to think clearly upon the Negro problem in all of its phases, and who have not only the breadth of intelligence to form just and generous opinions, but who possess that rarer quality, the courage to give them out openly to the country. General Morgan contributes the following article to the "New York Independent," analyzing the motives which underlie the color line in the army. He has had wide experience in military affairs, and his close contact with Negro soldiers during the Civil War entitles him to speak with authority. General Morgan says:

"The question of the color line has assumed an acute stage, and has called forth a good deal of feeling. The various Negro papers in the country are very generally insisting that if the Negro soldiers are to be enlisted, Negro officers should be appointed to command them. One zealous paper is clamoring for the appointment, immediately, by the President, of a Negro Major-General. The readers of "The Independent" know very well that during the Civil War there were enlisted in the United States army 200,000 Negro soldiers under white officers, the highest position assigned to a black man being that of first sergeant, or of regimental sergeant-major. The Negroes were allowed to wear chevrons, but not shoulder-straps or epaulets. Although four Negro regiments have been incorporated in the regular army, and have rendered exceptionally effective service on the plains and elsewhere for a whole generation, there are to-day no Negro officers in the service. A number of young men have been appointed as cadets at West Point, but the life has not been by any means an easy one. The only caste or class with caste distinctions that exists in the

Republic is found in the army; army officers are, par excellence, the aristocrats; nowhere is class feeling so much cultivated as among them; nowhere is it so difficult to break down the established lines. Singularly enough, though entrance to West Point is made very broad, and a large number of those who go there to be educated at the expense of the Government have no social position to begin with, and no claims to special merit, and yet, after having been educated at the public expense, and appointed to life positions, they seem to cherish the feeling that they are a select few, entitled to special consideration, and that they are called upon to guard their class against any insidious invasions. Of course there are honorable exceptions. There are many who have been educated at West Point who are broad in their sympathies, democratic in their ideas, and responsive to every appeal of philanthropy and humanity; but the spirit of West Point has been opposed to the admission of Negroes into the ranks of commissioned officers, and the opposition to the commissioning of black men emanating from the army will go very far toward the defeat of any project of that kind.

"To make the question of the admission of Negroes into the higher ranks of commissioned officers more difficult is the fact that the organization of Negro troops under the call of the President for volunteers to carry on the war with Spain has been left chiefly to the Governors of States. Very naturally the strong public sentiment against the Negro, which obtains almost universally in the South, has thus far prevented the recognition of his right to be treated precisely as the white man is treated. It would be, indeed, almost revolutionary for any Southern Governor to commission a Negro as a colonel of a regiment, or even a captain of a company. (Since this was written two Negro colonels have been appointed—in the Third North Carolina and Eighth Illinois.) Even where there are exceptions to this rule, they are notable exceptions. Everywhere through the South Negro volunteers are made to feel that they are not upon the same plane as white volunteers.

"In a recent conversation with the Adjutant-General of the Army, I was assured by him that in the organization of the ten regiments of immunes which Congress has authorized, the President had decided that five of them should be composed of Negroes, and that while the field and staff officers and captains are to be white, the lieutenants may be Negroes. If this is done it will mark a distinct step in advance of any taken hitherto. It will recognize partially, at least, the manhood of the Negro, and break down that unnatural bar of separation now existing. If a Negro is a lieutenant, he will command his company in the

absence of the captain. He can wear epaulets
and be entitled to all the rights and privileges
'of an officer and a gentleman'; he is no longer
doomed to inferiority. In case of battle, where
bullets have no respect of persons, and do not
draw the line at color, it may easily happen
that a regiment or battalion will do its best
work in the face of the enemy under the command of a Negro chief. Thus far the Government has been swift to recognize heroism and
efficiency, whether performed by Commodore
Dewey at Manila or Lieutenant Hobson at
Santiago, and it can hardly be otherwise than
that it will be ready to recognize exceptional
prowess and skill when performed by a Negro
officer.

"All, perhaps, which the Negroes themselves,
or their friends, have a right to ask in their
behalf is, that they shall have a chance to show
the stuff they are made of. The immortal
Lincoln gave them this chance when he admitted them to wear the blue and carry a musket;
and right manfully did they justify his confidence. There was not better fighting done
during the Civil War than was done by some
of the Negro troops. With my experience, in
command of 5,000 Negro soldiers, I would, on
the whole, prefer, I think, the command of a
corps of Negro troops to that of a corps of
white troops. With the magnificent record of
their fighting qualities on many a hard-con-

tested field, it is not unreasonable to ask that a still further opportunity shall be extended to them in commissioning them as officers, as well as enlisting them as soldiers.

"Naturally and necessarily the question of fitness for official responsibility is the prime test and ought to be applied, and if Negroes cannot be found of sufficient intelligence or preparation for the duties incumbent on army officers, nobody should object to the places being given to qualified white men. But so long as we draw no race line of distinction as against Germans or Irishmen, and institute no test of religion, politics or culture, we ought not to erect an artificial barrier of color. If the Negroes are competent they should be commissioned. If they are incompetent they should not be trusted with the grave responsibilities attached to official position. I believe they are competent."

CHAPTER V.

MANY TESTIMONIALS IN BEHALF OF THE NEGRO SOLDIERS.

A SOUTHERNER'S STATEMENT, THAT THE NEGRO CAVALRY SAVED THE "ROUGH RIDERS."

Some of the officers who accompanied the wounded soldiers on the trip north give interesting accounts of the fighting around Santiago. "I was standing near Captain Capron and Hamilton Fish, Jr.," said a corporal to the "Associated Press" correspondent to-night, "and saw them shot down. They were with the Rough Riders and ran into an ambuscade, though they had been warned of the danger. If it had not been for the Negro Cavalry the Rough Riders would have been exterminated. I am not a Negro lover. My father fought with Mosby's Rangers, and I was born in the South, but the Negroes saved that fight, and the day will come when General Shafter will give them credit for their bravery."—"Associated Press."

RECONCILIATION.

"Members of our regiment kicked somewhat when the colored troops were sent forward with them, but when they saw how the Negroes fought they became reconciled to the situation and some of them now say the colored brother can have half of their blankets whenever they want them."

The above is an extract from a communication to the "Daily Afternoon Journal," of Beaumont, Tex., written by a Southern white soldier. "Straws tell the way the wind blows," is a hackneyed expression, but an apt illustration of the subject in hand. It has been hinted by a portion of the Negro press that when the war ended, that if there is to be the millennium of North and South, the Negroes will suffer in the contraction. There is no reason to encourage this pessimistic view, since it is so disturbing in its nature, and since it is in the province of the individuals composing the race to create a future to more or less extent. The wedge has entered; it remains for the race to live up to its opportunities. The South already is making concessions. While concessions are apt to be looked upon as too patronizing, and not included in the classification of rights in common, yet in time they amount to the same. The mere statement that "the colored brother can have half of their blankets whenever they want them," while doubtless a figure of speech, yet it signifies under this very extreme of speech an appreciable advance of the race. It does not mean that there is to be a storming of the social barriers, for even in the more favored races definite lines are drawn. Sets and circles adjust such matters. But what is desired is the toleration of the Negroes in those pursuits that the people engage in or enjoy in general and in common. It is all that the American Negro may expect, and it is safe to say that his ambitions do not run higher, and ought not to run higher. Money and birth in themselves have created some unwritten laws that are much stronger than those decreed and promulgated by governments. It would be the height of presumption to strike at these, to some extent, privileged classes. It is to be hoped that the good fortunes of war will produce sanity and stability in the race, contending for abstract justice.—"Freeman."

The testimony continues:

Private Smith of the Seventy-first Volunteers, speaking about the impression his experience at Santiago had made upon him, said:

"I am a Southerner by birth, and I never thought much of the colored man. But, somehow, now I feel very differently toward them, for I met them in camp, on the battlefield, and that's where a man gets to know a man. I never saw such fighting as those Tenth Cavalry men did. They didn't seem to know what fear was, and their battle hymn was, 'There'll be a hot time in the old town to-night.' That's not a thrilling hymn to hear on the concert stage, but when you are lying in a trench with the smell of powder in your nose and the crack of rifles almost deafening you, and bullets tearing up the ground around you like huge hailstones beating down the dirt, and you see before you a blockhouse from which there belches forth the machine gun, pouring a torrent of leaden missiles, while from holes in the ground you see the leveled rifles of thousands of enemies that crack out death in ever-increasing succession, and then you see a body of men go up that hill as if it were in drill, so solid do they keep their formation, and those men are yelling, 'There'll be a hot time in the old town to-night,' singing as if they like their work, why, there's an appropriateness in the tune that kind of makes your blood creep and your nerves to thrill, and you want to get up and go ahead if you lose a limb in the attempt. And that's what those 'niggers' did. You just heard the Lieutenant say, 'Men, will you follow me?' and you hear a tremendous shout answer him, 'You bet we will,' and right up through that death-dealing storm you see men charge, that is, you see them until the darned Snider rifle powder blinds you and hides them.

"And there is another thing, too, that teaches a man a lesson. The action of the officers on the field is what I speak of. Somehow when you watch these men with their gold braid in armories on a dance night or dress parade it strikes you that they are a little more handsome and ornamental than they are practical and

General Maximo Gomez, of the Cuban Army.

useful. To tell the truth, I didn't think much of those dandy officers on parade or dancing round a ballroom. I did not really think they were worth the money that was spent upon them. But I just found it was different on the battlefield, and they just knew their business and bullets were a part of the show to them."

NEGRO SOLDIERS.

The Charleston "News and Courier" says:

"It is not known what proportion of the insurgent army is colored, but the indications are that the proportion of the same element in the volunteer army of occupation will be small.

"On the basis of population, of course, one-third of the South's quota should be made up of colored, and it is to be remembered that they made good soldiers and constitute a large part of the regular army. There were nearly 250,000 of them in service in the last war."

THE NEGRO AS A SOLDIER—HIS GOOD MARKSMANSHIP—THE FIGHT AT EL CANEY—"WOE TO SPAN-ISH IN RANGE."

There has been hitherto among the officers of the army a certain prejudice against serving in the Negro regiments. But the other day a Lieutenant in the Ninth Infantry said enthusiastically:

"Do you know, I shouldn't want anything

better than to have a company in a Negro
regiment? I am from Virginia, and have
always had the usual feeling about commanding colored troops. But after seeing that
charge of the Twenty-fourth up the San Juan
Hill, I should like the best in the world to
have a Negro company. They went up that
incline yelling and shouting just as I used to
hear when they were hunting rabbits in Virginia. The Spanish bullets only made them
wilder to reach the trenches."

Officers of other regiments which were near
the Twenty-fourth on July 1st are equally
strong in their praise of the Negroes. Their
yells were an inspiration to their white comrades and spread dismay among the Spaniards.
A captain in a volunteer regiment declares that
the Twenty-fourth did more than any other
to win the day at San Juan. As they charged
up through the white soldiers their enthusiasm
was spread, and the entire line fought the better for their cheers and their wild rush.

Spanish evidence to the effectiveness of the
colored soldiers is not lacking. Thus an officer
who was with the troops that lay in wait for the
Americans at La Guasima on June 24th, said:

"What especially terrified our men was the
huge American Negroes. We saw their big,
black faces through the underbrush, and they
looked like devils. They came forward under
our fire as if they didn't the least care about it."

THE CHARGE AT EL CANEY.

It was the Tenth Cavalry that had this effect on the Spaniards. At San Juan the Ninth Cavalry distinguished itself, its commander, Lieutenant-Colonel Hamilton, being killed. The fourth of the Negro regiments, the Twenty-fifth Infantry, played an especially brilliant part in the battle of El Caney on July 1st. It was held in reserve with the rest of Colonel Miles' brigade, but was ordered to support General Lawton's brigade toward the middle of the day. At that hour marching was an ordeal, but the men went on at a fast pace. With almost no rest they kept it up until they got into action. The other troops had been fighting hard for hours, and the arrival of the Twenty-fifth was a blessing. The Negroes went right ahead through the tired ranks of their comrades. Their charge up the hill, which was surmounted by Spanish rifle pits and a stone fort, has been told. It was the work of only a part of the regiment, the men coming chiefly from three companies. Colonel Miles had intended having his whole brigade make the final charge, but the Twenty-fifth didn't wait for orders. It was there to take that hill, and take the hill it did.

One of the Spanish officers captured there seemed to think that the Americans were taking an unfair advantage of them in having colored men who fought like that. He had been accustomed to the Negroes in the insurgent army, and a different lot they are from those in the United States army.

"Why," he said ruefully, "even your Negroes fight better than any other troops I ever saw."

The way the Negroes charged up the El Caney and San Juan hills suggested inevitably that their African nature has not been entirely eliminated by generations of civilization, but was bursting forth in savage yells and in that wild rush, some of them were fairly frantic with the delight of the battle. And it was no mere craziness. They are excellent marksmen, and they aim carefully and well. Woe to the Spaniards who showed themselves above the trenches when a colored regiment was in good range.

MAGNIFICENT SHOWING MADE BY THE NEGROES—THEIR SPLENDID COURAGE AT SANTIAGO THE ADMIRATION OF ALL OFFI- CERS.

THEY WERE LED BY SOUTHERN MEN—BLACK MEN FROM THE SOUTH FOUGHT LIKE TIGERS AND END A QUESTION OFTEN DEBATED—IN ONLY ONE OR TWO ACTIONS OF THE CIVIL WAR WAS THERE SUCH A LOSS OF OFFICERS AS AT SAN JUAN.

[Telegram to "Commercial."]

Washington, July 6, 1898.

Veterans who are comparing the losses at the battle of San Juan, near Santiago, last Friday, with those at Big Bethel and the first

Bull Run say that in only one or two actions of the late war was there such a loss in officers as occurred at San Juan Hill.

The companies of the Twenty-fourth Infantry are without officers. The regiment had four captains knocked down within a minute of each other. Capt. A. C. Ducat was the first officer hit in the action, and was killed instantly. His second lieutenant, John A. Gurney, a Michigan man, was struck dead at the same time as the captain, and Lieutenant Henry G. Lyon was left in command of Company D, but only for a few minutes, for he, too, went down. Liscum, commanding the regiment, was killed.

NEGROES FIGHT LIKE TIGERS.

Company F, Twenty-fourth Infantry, lost Lieutenant Augustin, of Louisiana, killed, and Captain Crane was left without a commissioned officer. The magnificent courage of the Mississippi, Louisiana, Arkansas and Texas Negroes, which make up the rank and file of this regiment, is the admiration of every officer who has written here since the fight. The regiment has a large proportion of Southern-born officers, who led their men with more than usual exposure.

These men had always said the Southern Negro would fight as staunchly as any white man, if he was led by those in whom he had confidence. The question has often been de-

First Pay-Day in Cuba for the Ninth and Tenth Cavalry.

bated in every mess of the army. San Juan Hill offered the first occasion in which this theory could be tested practically, and tested it was in a manner and with a result that makes its believers proud of the men they commanded. It has helped the morale of the four Negro regiments beyond words. The men of the Twenty-fourth Infantry, particularly, and their comrades of the Ninth and Tenth Cavalry as well, are proud of the record they made.

THEY NEVER WAVERED.

The Twenty-fourth took the brunt of the fight, and all through it, even when whole companies were left without an officer, not for a moment were these colored soldiers shaken or wavering in the face of the fierce attack made upon them. Wounded Spanish officers declare that the attack was thus directed because they did not believe the Negro would stand up against them and they believed there was the faulty place in the American line. Never were men more amazed than were the Spanish officers to see the steadiness and cool courage with which the Twenty-fourth charged front forward on its tenth company (a difficult thing to do at any time), under the hottest fire. The value of the Negro as a soldier is no longer a debatable question. It has been proven fully in one of the sharpest fights of the past three years.

"OUR BOYS," THE SOLDIERS.

WHAT ARMY OFFICERS AND OTHERS HAVE TO SAY OF THE
NEGROES' CONDUCT IN WAR—"GIVE HONOR TO WHOM
HONOR IS DUE"—ACME OF BRAVERY.

It has been said, "Give honor to whom honor
is due," and while it is just and right that it
should be so, there are times, however, when
the "honor" due is withheld.

Ever since the battle of San Juan Hill at
Santiago de Cuba nearly every paper in the
land has had nothing but praise for the bravery
shown by the "Rough Riders," and to the extent that, not knowing the truth, one would
naturally arrive at the conclusion that the
"Rough Riders" were "the whole thing." Although sometimes delayed, the truth, like murder, "will out." It is well enough to praise
the "Rough Riders" for all they did, but why
not divide honors with the other fellows who
made it possible for them, the "Rough Riders,"
to receive praise, and be honored by a generous
and valor-loving nation?

After the battles of El Caney and San Juan
Hill, many wounded American soldiers who
were able to travel were given furloughs to
their respective homes in the United States, and
Lieutenant Thomas Roberts, of this city, was
one of them. Shortly after Lieutenant Roberts
arrived in the city he was interviewed by a
representative of the "Illinois State Register,"
to whom he gave a description of the battle of

July 1st. He said: "On the night of June 30th the second squadron of the Tenth Cavalry did outpost duty. Daylight opened on the soon-to-be blood-sodden field on July 1st, and the Tenth was ordered to the front. First went the first squadron, followed soon after by the second, composed of Troops G, I, B and A. The Tenth Cavalry is composed of Negroes, commanded by white officers, and I have naught but the highest praise for the swarthy warriors on the field of carnage. Led by brave men, they will go into the thickest of the fight, even to the wicket mouths of deadly cannon, unflinchingly."

Lieutenant Roberts says further that "at 9 o'clock on the morning of July 1st the order came to move. Forward we went, until we struck a road between two groves, which road was swept by a hail of shot and shell from Spanish guns. The men stood their ground as if on dress parade. Single file, every man ready to obey any command, they bade defiance to the fiercest storm of leaden hail that ever hurtled over a troop of United States cavalry. The order came, 'Get under cover,' and the Seventy-first New York and the Tenth Cavalry took opposite sides of the road and lay down in the bushes. For a short time no orders came, and feeling a misapprehension of the issue, I hastened forward to consult with the first lieutenant of the company. We found that through a misinterpreted order the captain of the troop and eight men had gone forward. Hastening back to my post I consulted with the captain in the rear of Troop G, and the quartermaster appeared upon the scene asking the whereabouts of the Tenth Cavalry. They made known their presence, and the quartermaster told them to go on. Showing the path, the quartermaster led them forward until the bend in the San Juan River was reached. Here the first bloodshed in the Tenth occurred, a young volunteer named Baldwin fell, pierced by a Spanish ball."

An aide hastened up and gave the colonel of the regiment orders to move forward. The summit of the hill was crowned by two blockhouses, and from these came an unceasing fire. Lieutenant Roberts said he had been lying on the ground, but rose to his knees to repeat an order, "Move forward," when a mauser ball struck him in the abdomen and passed entirely through his body. Being wounded, he was carried off the field, but after all was over, Lieutenant Roberts says it was said (on the quiet, of course) that "the heroic charge of the Tenth Cavalry saved the 'Rough Riders' from destruction." Lieutenant Roberts says he left Cuba on the 12th of July for Fort Monroe, and that a wounded Rough Rider told him while coming over that "had it not been for the Tenth Cavalry the Rough Riders would never have passed through the seething caldron of Spanish missiles." Such is the statement of one of Spring-field's best citizens, a member of the Tenth Cavalry, United States regulars.

Some days later, Lieutenant Roberts had occasion to visit Chicago and Fort Sheridan, and while there he was interviewed by a repre-sentative of the "Chicago Chronicle," to whom he related practically the same story as above stated. "You probably know my regiment is made up exclusively of Negroes except for the commissioned officers, and I want to say right here that those men performed deeds of heroism on that day which have no parallel in the his-tory of warfare. They were under fire from six in the morning until 1:30 in the afternoon, with strict orders not to return the hail of lead, and not a man in those dusky ranks flinched. Our brigade was instructed to move forward soon after 1 o'clock to assault the series of blockhouses which was regarded as impregna-ble by the foreign attachés. As the aide dashed down our lines with orders from headquarters the boys realized the prayed-for charge was about to take place and cheered lustily. Such a charge! Will I ever forget that sublime spec-tacle? There was a river called San Juan, from the hill hard by, but which historians will term the pool of blood. Our brigade had to follow the course of that creek fully half a mile to reach the point selected for the grand attack. With what cheering did the boys go up that

First President of the Cuban Republic.

hill! Their naked bodies seemed to present a
perfect target to the fire of the dons, but they
never flinched. When the command reached
the famous stone blockhouse it was commanded
by a second sergeant, who was promoted on
the field of battle for extraordinary bravery.
San Juan fell many minutes before El Caney,
which was attacked first, and I think the Negro
soldiers can be thanked for the greater part
of that glorious work. All honor to the Negro
soldiers! No white man, no matter what his
ancestry may be, should be ashamed to greet
any of those Negro cavalrymen with out-
stretched hand. The swellest of the Rough
Riders counted our troopers among their best
friends and asked them to their places in New
York when they returned, and I believe the
wealthy fellows will prove their admiration had
a true inspiration."

Thus we see that while the various newspapers of the country are striving to give the
Rough Riders first honors, an honest, straight-
forward army officer who was there and took an
active part in the fight, does not hesitate to give
honor to whom honor is due, for he says, "All
honor to the Negro soldiers," and that it was
they who "saved the Rough Riders from destruction." And right here I wish to call the
reader's attention to another very important
matter, and that is, while it has been said heretofore that the Negro soldier was not competent

to command, do not the facts in the case prove, beyond a doubt, that there is no truth in the statement whatever? If a white colonel was "competent" to lead his command into the fight, it seems that a colored sergeant was competent extraordinary, for he not only went into the fight, but he, and his command, "done something," done the enemy out of the trenches, "saved the Rough Riders from destruction," and planted the Stars and Stripes on the blockhouse.

Just before the charge, one of the foreign attachés, an Englishman, was heard to say that he did not see how the blockhouse was to be reached without the aid of cannon; but after the feat had been accomplished, a colored soldier said, "We showed him how."

Now that the colored soldier has proven to this nation, and the representatives of others, that he can, and does fight, as well as the "other fellow," and that he is also "competent" to command, it remains to be seen if the national government will give honor to whom honor is due, by honoring those deserving with commissions. Under the second call for volunteers by the President, the State of Illinois raised a regiment of colored soldiers, and Governor Tanner officered that regiment with colored officers from colonel down; and that, as you might say, before they had earned their "rank." Now the question is, can the national government afford to do less by those who have earned, and are

justly entitled to, a place in the higher ranks?
We shall see.   C. F. ANDERSON.
    Springfield, Ill.   _____

COLORED FIGHTERS AT SANTIAGO.

Testimony is multiplying of the bravery of
the colored troops at Santiago de Cuba July 1st
and 2d, 1898.

Testimony is adduced to show that these
"marvels of warfare" actually fought without
officers and executed movements under a galling
fire which would have puzzled a recruit on
parade ground. The "Boston Journal" of the
31st, in its account, gives the following interview—Mason Mitchell (white) said:

"We were in a valley when we started, but
made at once for a trail running near the top
of a ridge called La Quasina, several hundred
feet high, which, with several others parallel to
it, extended in the direction of Santiago. By
a similar trail near the top of the ridge to our
right several companies of Negro troopers of
the Ninth and Tenth United States Cavalry
marched in scout formation, as we did. We
had an idea about where the Spaniards were
and depended upon Cuban scouts to warn us,
but they did not do it. At about 8.30 o'clock in
the morning we met a volley from the enemy,
who were ambushed, not only on our ridge, but
on the one to the right. Beyond the Negro
troops and the Negro soldiers were under a

cross fire. That is how Capt. Capron and Hamilton Fish were killed."

It says: "Handsome young Sergt. Stewart, the Rough Rider protégé of Henry W. Maxwell, when he was telling of the fight in the ambush, gave it as his opinion that the Rough Riders would have been wiped out if the tenth Cavalry (colored) had not come up just in time to drive the Spaniards back. 'I'm a Southerner, from New Mexico, and I never thought much of the "nigger" before. Now I know what they are made of. I respect them. They certainly can fight like the devil and they don't care for bullets any more than they do for the leaves that shower down on them. I've changed my opinion of the colored folks, for of all the men that I saw fighting, there were none to beat the Tenth Cavalry and the colored infantry at Santiago, and I don't mind saying so.'"

The description which follows is interesting:

"It was simply grand to see how those young fellows, and old fellows, too, men who were rich and had been the petted of society in the city, walk up and down the lines while their clothes were powdered by the dust from exploding shells and torn by broken fragments, cool as could be, and yelling to the men to lay low and take good aim, or directing some squad to take care of a poor devil who was wounded. Why, at times there when the bullets were so thick they mowed the grass down like grass cutters in places, the officers stood looking at the enemy through glasses as if they were enjoying the scene, and now and then you'd see a Captain or a Lieutenant pick up a gun from a wounded or dead man and blaze away himself at some good shot that he had caught sight of from his vantage point. Those sights kind of bring men together and make them think more of each other. And when a white man strayed from his regiment and falls wounded it rather affects him to have a Negro, shot himself a couple of times, take his carbine and make a splint of it to keep a torn limb together for the white soldier, and then, after lifting him to one side, pick up the wounded man's rifle and go back to the fight with as much vigor as ever. Yes, sir, we boys have learned something down there, even if some of us were pretty badly torn for it."

Another witness testifies: "Trooper Lewis Bowman, another of the brave Tenth Cavalry, had two ribs broken by a Spanish shell while before San Juan. He told of the battle as follows:

"'The Rough Riders had gone off in great glee, bantering up and good-naturedly boasting that they were going ahead to lick the Spaniards without any trouble, and advising us to remain where we were until they returned, and they would bring back some Spanish heads as trophies. When we heard firing in the distance, our Captain remarked that some one ahead

was doing good work. The firing became so
heavy and regular that our officers, without
orders, decided to move forward and recon-
noitre. When we got where we could see what
was going on we found that the Rough Riders
had marched down a sort of canyon between
the mountains. The Spaniards had men posted
at the entrance, and, as soon as the Rough
Riders had gone in, had about closed up the
rear and were firing upon the Rough Riders
from both the front and rear. Immediately
the Spaniards in the rear received a volley from
our men of the Tenth Cavalry (colored) without command. The Spaniards were afraid we
were going to flank them, and rushed out of
ambush, in front of the Rough Riders, throw-
ing up their hands and shouting, "Don't shoot;
we are Cubans."

"'The Rough Riders thus let them escape,
and gave them a chance to take a better position ahead. During all this time the men were
all in the tall grass and could not see even each
other, a·d I feared the Rough Riders in the
rear shot many of their men in the front, mis-
taking them for Spanish soldiers. By this time
the Tenth Cavalry had fully taken in the situation, and, adopting the method employed in
fighting the Indians, were able to turn the tide
of battle and repulse the Spaniards.'"

He speaks plainly when he says:

"I don't think it an exaggeration to say that

if it had not been for the timely aid of the Tenth Cavalry (colored) the Rough Riders would have been exterminated. This is the unanimous opinion, at least, of the men of the Tenth Cavalry. I was in the fight of July 1, and it was in that fight that I received my wound. We were under fire in that fight about forty-eight hours, and were without food and with but little water. We had been cut off from our pack train, as the Spanish sharpshooters shot our mules as soon as they came anywhere near the lines, and it was impossible to move supplies. Very soon after the firing began our Colonel was killed, and the most of our other officers were killed or wounded, so that the greater part of that desperate battle was fought by some of the Ninth and Tenth Cavalry without officers; or, at least, if there were any officers around, we neither saw them nor heard their commands. The last command I heard our Captain give was:

" 'Boys, when you hear my whistle, lie flat down on the ground.'

"Whether he ever whistled or not I do not know. The next move we made was when, with a terrific yell, we charged up to the Spanish trenches and bayoneted and clubbed them out of their places in a jiffy. Some of the men of our regiment say that the last command they heard was: 'To the rear!' But this command they utterly disregarded and charged to the front until the day was won, and the Spaniards, those not dead in the trenches, fled back to the city."

But a colored man, Wm. H. Brown, a member of the Tenth Cavalry, said:

"A foreign officer, standing near our position when we started out to make that charge, was heard to say: 'Men, for heaven's sake don't go up that hill! It will be impossible for human beings to take that position! You can't stand the fire!' Notwithstanding this, with a terrific yell we rushed up the enemy's works, and you know the result. Men who saw him say that when this officer saw us make the charge he turned his back upon us and wept.

"And the odd thing about it all is that these wounded heroes never will admit that they did anything out of the common. They will talk all right about those 'other fellows,' but they don't about themselves, and were immensely surprised when such a fuss was made over them on their arrival and since. They simply believed they had a duty to perform and performed it." —"Planet."

OUR COLORED SOLDIERS.

A FEW OF THE INTERESTING COMMENTS ON THE DEEDS PERFORMED BY THE BRAVE BOYS OF THE REGULAR ARMY—SAVED THE LIFE OF HIS LIEUTENANT BUT LOST HIS OWN.

"The Ninth and Tenth Cavalry are composed of the bravest lot of soldiers I ever saw. They held the ground that Roosevelt retreated from and saved them from annihilation."

To a Massachusetts soldier in another group of interviewers, the same question was put: "How about the colored soldiers?"

"They fought like demons," came the answer.

"Before El Caney was taken the Spaniards were on the heights of San Juan with heavy guns. All along our line an assault was made and the enemy was holding us off with terrible effect. From their blockhouse on the hill came a magazine of shot. Shrapnell shells fell in our ranks, doing great damage. Something had to be done or the day would have been lost. The Ninth and part of the Tenth Cavalry moved across into a thicket near by. The Spaniards rained shot upon them. They collected and like a flash swept across the plains and charged up the hill. The enemy's guns were used with deadly effect. On and on they went, charging with the fury of madness. The blockhouse was captured, the enemy fled and we went into El Caney."

In another group a trooper from an Illinois regiment was explaining the character of the country and the effect of the daily rains upon the troops. Said he:

"Very few colored troops are sick. They stood the climate better and even thrived on the severity of army life."

Said he: "I never had much use for a 'nigger'

Cubans Fighting from Tree Tops.

and didn't want him in the fight. He is all right, though. He makes a good soldier and deserves great credit."

Another comrade near by related the story as told by a cavalry lieutenant, who with a party reconnoitered a distance from camp. The thick growth of grass and vines made ambuscading a favorite pastime with the Spaniards. With smokeless powder they lay concealed in the grass. As the party rode along the sharp eye of a colored cavalryman noticed the movement of grass ahead. Leaning over his horse with sword in hand he plucked up an enemy whose gun was levelled at the officer. The Spaniard was killed by the Negro, who himself fell dead, shot by another. He had saved the life of his lieutenant and lost his own.

A comrade of the Seventeenth Infantry gave his testimony. Said he:

"I shall never forget the 1st of July. At one time in the engagement of that day the Twenty-first Infantry had faced a superior force of Spaniards and were almost completely surrounded. The Twenty-fourth Infantry, of colored troops, seeing the perilous position of the Twenty-first, rushed to the rescue, charged and routed the enemy, thereby saving the ill-fated regiment."

Col. Joseph Haskett, of the Seventeenth Regular Infantry, testifies to the meritorious conduct of the Negro troops. Said he:

"Our colored soldier is 100 per cent. superior to the Cuban. He is a good scout, brave soldier, and not only that, but is everywhere to be seen building roads for the movement of heavy guns."

Among the trophies of war brought to Old Point were a machete, the captured property of a colored trooper, and a fine Spanish sword, taken from an officer, and a little Cuban lad about nine years old, whose parents had bled for Cuba. His language and appearance made him the cynosure of all eyes. He was dressed in a little United States uniform and had pinned to his clothing a tag which read: "Santiago buck, care of Col. C. L. Wilson, Manhattan Club, New York." His name is Varrames y Pillero.

He seemed to enjoy the shower of small coin that fell upon him from the hotels. His first and only English words were "Moocha Moona."

These fragments were gathered while visiting at Old Point Comfort. They serve to show the true feeling of the whites for their brave black brother.

A. E. MEYZEEK, in the "Freeman."

Louisville, Ky.

BLACK SOLDIER BOYS.

The following is what the New York "Mail and Express" said respecting the good services being rendered by our black soldier boys:

"All honors to the black troopers of the gallant Tenth! No more striking example of bravery and coolness has been shown since the destruction of the Maine than by the colored veterans of the Tenth Cavalry during the attack upon Caney on Saturday. By the side of the intrepid Rough Riders they followed their leader up the terrible hill from whose crest the desperate Spaniards poured down a deadly fire of shell and musketry. They never faltered. The breaks in their ranks were filled as soon as made. Firing as they charged, their aim was splendid, their coolness was superb, and their courage aroused the admiration of their comrades. Their advance was greeted with wild cheers from the white regiments, and with an answering shout they pressed onward over the trenches they had taken close in the pursuit of the retreating enemy. The war has not shown greater heroism. The men whose own freedom was baptized with blood have proved themselves capable of giving up their lives that others may be free. To-day is a glorious Fourth for all races of people in this great land."

THEY NEVER FALTERED.

The test of the Negro soldier has been applied and to-day the whole world stands amazed at the valor and distinctive bravery shown by the men, who, in the face of a most galling fire, rushed onward while shot and shell tore fearful gaps in their ranks. These men, the Tenth Cavalry, did not stop to ask was it worth while for them to lay down their lives for the honor of a country that has silently allowed her citizens to be killed and maltreated in almost every conceivable way; they did not stop to ask would their death bring deliverance to their race from mob violence and lynching. They saw their duty and did it! The "New York Journal" catches inspiration from the wonderful courage of the Tenth Cavalry and writes these words:

"The two most picturesque and most characteristically American commands in General Shafter's army bore off the great honors of a day in which all won honor.

"No man can read the story in to-day's 'Journal' of the 'Rough Riders'' charge on the blockhouse at El Caney, of Theodore Roosevelt's mad daring in the face of what seemed certain death, without having his pulses beat faster and some reflected light of the fire of battle gleam from his eyes.

"And over against this scene of the cowboy and the college graduate, the New York man about town and the Arizona bad man united in one coherent war machine, set the picture of the Tenth United States Cavalry—the famous colored regiment. Side by side with Roosevelt's men they fought—these black men. Scarce used to freedom themselves, they are dying that Cuba may be free. Their marksmanship was magnificent, say the eyewitnesses. Their courage was superb. They bore themselves like veterans, and gave proof positive that out of nature naturally peaceful, careless and playful, military discipline and an inspiring cause can make soldiers worthy to rank with Caesar's legions or Cromwell's army.

"The Rough Riders and the Black Regiment! In those two commands is an epitome of almost our whole national character."

THE NEGRO AS A SOLDIER.

HIS GOOD NATURE—HIS KINDHEARTEDNESS—EQUALLY AVAILABLE IN INFANTRY OR CAVALRY.

The good nature of the Negro soldier is remarkable. He is always fond of a joke and never too tired to enjoy one. Officers have wondered to see a whole company of them, at the close of a long practice march, made with heavy baggage, chasing a rabbit which some one may have started. They will run for several hundred yards whooping and yelling and laughing, and come back to camp feeling as if they had had lots of fun. The white soldier, even if not tired, would never see any joke in rushing after a rabbit. To the colored man the diversion is a delight.

In caring for the sick, the Negro's tenderheartedness is conspicuous. On one of the transports loaded with sick men a white soldier asked to be helped to his bunk below. No one of his color stirred, but two Negro convalescents at once went to his assistance. When volunteers were called for to cook for the sick, only Negroes responded. They were pleased to be of service to their officers. If the Captain's child is ill, every man in the company is solicitous; half of them want to act as nurse. They feel honored to be hired to look after an officer's horse and clothing. The "striker," as he is called, soon gets to look on himself as a part of his master; it is no "Captain has been ordered away," but "We have been ordered away." Every concern of his employer about which he knows interests him, and a slight to his superior is vastly more of an offence than if offered to himself. Indeed, if the army knew how well officers of the colored regiments are looked after by their men, there would be less disinclination to serve in such commands. After years with a Negro company, officers find it difficult to get along with white soldiers. They must be much more careful to avoid hurting sensibilities, and must do without many little services to which they have been accustomed.

MRS. PORTER'S RIDE TO THE FRONT.

For many years she has known and admired Miss Barton, and against the advice of her friends had resolved to help Miss Barton in her task of succoring the sufferers in Cuba.

During the second day's fighting Mrs. Porter, escorted by a general whom she has known for many years, rode almost to the firing line. Bullets whistled about her head, but she rode bravely on until her curiosity was satisfied. Then she rode leisurely back to safety. She came back filled with admiration of the colored troops. She described them as being "brave in battle, obedient under orders and philosophical under privations."

Thanks to Mrs. Porter, the wife of the President's private secretary. Mrs. Porter is one of heaven's blessings, sent as a messenger of "The Ship" earth, to testify in America what she saw of the Negro troops in Cuba.

THE INVESTMENT OF SANTIAGO AND SURRENDER.

(As Presented in the "N. Y. World.")

General Shafter put a human rope of 22,400 men around Santiago, with its 26,000 Spanish soldiers, and then Spain succumbed in despair. In a semicircle extending around Santiago, from Daiquiri on the east clear around to Cobre on the west, our troops were stretched a cordon of almost impenetrable thickness and strength. First came General Bates, with the Ninth, Tenth, Third, Thirteenth, Twenty-first and Twenty-fourth U. S. Infantry. On his right crouched General Sumner, commanding the Third, Sixth and Ninth U. S. Cavalry. Next

Investment of Santiago by U. S. Army.

along the arc were the Seventh, Twelfth and
Seventeenth U. S. Infantry under General
Chaffee. Then, advantageously posted, there
were six batteries of artillery prepared to sweep
the horizon under direction of General Randolph. General Jacob Kent, with the Seventy-
first New York Volunteers and the Sixth and
Sixteenth U. S. Infantry, held the centre. They
were flanked by General Wheeler and the
Rough Riders, dismounted; eight troops of the
First U. S. Volunteers, four troops of the Second U. S. Cavalry, four light batteries, two
heavy batteries and then four more troops of
the Second U. S. Cavalry.

SANTIAGO'S KILLED AND WOUNDED COMPARED WITH HISTORIC
BATTLES.

	Men Engaged	Killed and Wounded.	Lost. Per Ct.
Agincourt	62,000	11,400	.18
Alma	103,000	8,400	.08
Bannockburn	135,000	38,000	.28
Borodino	250,000	78,000	.31
Cannæ	146,000	52,000	.34
Cressy	117,000	31,000	.27
Gravelotte	396,000	62,000	.16
Sadowa	291,000	33,000	.11
Waterloo	221,000	51,000	.23
Antietam	87,000	31,000	.29
Austerlitz	154,000	38,000	.48
Gettysburg	185,000	34,000	.44
Sedan	314,000	47,000	.36
Santiago	22,400	1,457	.07
{ El Caney	3,300	650	.19
{ San Juan	6,000	745	.12
{ Aguadores	2,400	62	.02

General Lawton, with the Second Massachusetts and the Eighth and Twenty-second U. S. Infantry, came next. Then General Duffield's command, comprising the volunteers from Michigan (Thirty-third and Third Regiments), and the Ninth Massachusetts, stretched along until General Ludlow's men were reached. These comprised the First Illinois, First District of Columbia, Eighth Ohio, running up to the Eighth and Twenty-second Regulars and the Bay State men. Down by the shore across from Morro and a little way inland Generals Henry and Garretson had posted the Sixth Illinois and the crack Sixth Massachusetts, flanking the railroad line to Cobre.

SCENES OF THE FINAL SURRENDER.

When reveille sounded Sunday morning half the great semilunar camp was awake and eager for the triumphal entrance into the city. Speculation ran rife as to which detachment would accompany the General and his staff into Santiago. The choice fell upon the Ninth Infantry. Shortly before 9 o'clock General Shafter left his headquarters, accompanied by Generals Lawton and Wheeler, Colonels Ludlow, Ames and Kent, and eighty other officers. The party walked slowly down the hill to the road leading to Santiago, along which they advanced until they reached the now famous tree outside the walls, under which all negotiations for the surrender of the city had taken place. As they reached this spot the cannon on every hillside and in the city itself boomed forth a salute of twenty-one guns, which was echoed at Siboney and Aserradero.

The soldiers knew what the salute meant, and cheer upon cheer arose and ran from end to end of the eight miles of the American lines. A troop of colored cavalry and the Twenty-fifth Colored Infantry then started to join General Shafter and his party.

The Americans waited under the tree as usual, when General Shafter sent word to General Toral that he was ready to take possession of the town. General Toral, in full uniform, accompanied by his whole staff, fully caparisoned, shortly afterward left the city and walked to where the American officers were waiting their coming. When they reached the tree General Shafter and General Toral saluted each other gravely and courteously. Salutes were also exchanged by other American and Spanish officers. The officers were then introduced to each other. After this little ceremony the two commanding generals faced each other and General Toral, speaking in Spanish, said:

"Through fate I am forced to surrender to General Shafter, of the American Army, the city and the strongholds of Santiago."

General Toral's voice grew husky as he spoke,

giving up the town and the surrounding country to his victorious enemy. As he finished speaking the Spanish officers presented arms.

General Shafter, in reply, said:

"I receive the city in the name of the government of the United States."

General Toral addressed an order to his officers in Spanish and they wheeled about, still presenting arms, and General Shafter and the other American officers, with the cavalry and infantry, followed them, walked by the Spaniards and proceeded into the city proper.

The soldiers on the American line could see quite plainly all the proceedings. As their commander entered the city they gave voice to cheer after cheer.

Although no attempt was made to humiliate them, the Spanish soldiers seemed at first to feel downcast and scarcely glanced at their conquerors as they passed by, but this apparent depth of feeling was not displayed very long. Without being sullen they appeared to be utterly indifferent to the reverses of the Spanish arms, but it was not long ere the prospect of regulation rations and a chance to go to their homes made them almost cheerful. All about the filthy streets of the city the starving refugees could be seen, gaunt, hollow-eyed, weak and trembling.

The squalor in the streets was dreadful. The bones of dead horses and other animals were bleaching in the streets and buzzards almost as tame as sparrows hopped aside as passers-by disturbed them. There was a fetid smell everywhere and evidences of a pitiless siege and starvation on every hand.

The palace was reached soon after 10 o'clock. Then General Toral introduced General Shafter and the other officials to various local dignitaries and a scanty luncheon was brought. Coffee, rice, wine and toasted cake were the main condiments.

Then came the stirring scene in the balcony which every one felt was destined to become notably historic in our annals of warfare, and the ceremony over, General Shafter withdrew to our own lines and left the city to General McKibbin and his police force of guards and sentries. The end had come. Spain's haughty. ensign trailed in the dust; Old Glory, typifying liberty and the pursuit of happiness untrammelled floated over the official buildings from Fort Morro to the Plaza de Armas—the investment of Santiago de Cuba was accomplished.

General Russell A. Alger, Secretary of War.

CHAPTER VI.

NO COLOR LINE DRAWN IN CUBA.

A GRAPHIC DESCRIPTION—CONDITIONS IN THE PEARL OF
THE ANTILLES—AMERICAN PREJUDICE CANNOT EXIST
THERE—A CATHOLIC PRIEST VOUCHES FOR THE
ACCURACY OF STATEMENT.

The article we reprint from the "New York Sun" touching the status of the Colored man in Cuba was shown to Rev. Father Walter R. Yates, assistant pastor of St. Joseph's Colored Church.

A "Planet" reporter was informed that Father Yates had resided in that climate for several years and wished his views.

"The 'Sun' correspondent is substantially correct," said the reverend gentleman. "Of course, the article is very incomplete, there are many omissions, but that is to be expected in a newspaper article.

"It would take volumes to describe the achievements of men of the Negro, or as I prefer to call it, the Aethiopic race, not only in Cuba, but in all the West Indies, Central and South America, and in Europe, especially in Sicily, Spain and France.

"By achievements I mean success in military, political, social, religious and literary walks of life. The only thing I see to correct in the

'Sun's' article," continued the Father, "is in regard to population. A Spanish official told me that the census figures were notoriously misleading. The census shows less than one-third colored. That is said not to be true. As soon as a man with African blood, whether light or dark, acquires property and education, he returns himself in the census as white. The officials humor them in this petty vanity. In fact, it's the most difficult thing in the world to distinguish between races in Cuba. Many Spaniards from Murcia, for instance, of undoubted noble lineage, are darker than Richmond mulatoes."

"May I ask you, Father Yates, to what do you ascribe the absence of race prejudice in Cuba?"

"Certainly. In my humble opinion it is due to Church influence. We all know the effect on our social life of our churches. Among Catholics all men have always been on equal footing at the Communion rail. Catholics would be unworthy of their name, i. e., Catholic or universal, were it not so.

"Even in the days when slavery was practised this religious equality and fellowship was fully recognized among Catholics.

"Did you know there is an American Negro saint? He was born in Colon, Central America, and is called Blessed Martin De Porres. His name is much honored in Cuba, Peru, Mexico and elsewhere. He wore the white habit of a Dominican Brother. The Dominicans are called the Order of Preachers.

"Christ Died for All. Father Donovan has those words painted in large letters over the Sanctuary in St. Joseph's Church. It is simply horrible to think that some self-styled Christian sectarians act as if Christ died for white men only."

Matanzas, Cuba, January 20.—Not least among the problems of reconstruction in Cuba is the social and political status of the colored "man and brother." In Cuba the shade of a man's complexion has never been greatly considered, and one finds dusky Othellos in every walk of life. The present dispute arose when a restaurant keeper from Alabama refused a seat at his public table to the mulatto Colonel of a Cuban regiment. The Southerner was perfectly sincere in the declaration that he would see himself in a warmer climate than Cuba before he would insult his American guests "by seating a 'nigger' among them!" To the Colonel it was a novel and astonishing experience, and is, of course, deeply resented by all his kind in Cuba, where African blood may be found, in greater or less degree, in some of the richest and most influential families of the Island.

COLORED BELLES THERE.

In Havana you need not be surprised to see Creole belles on the fashionable Prado—perhaps

Cuban-Spanish. Cuban-English or Cuban-German blondes—promenading with Negro officers in gorgeous uniforms; or octoroon beauties with hair in natural crimp, riding in carriages beside white husbands or lighting up an opera box with the splendor of their diamonds. There was a wedding in the old cathedral the other day, attended by the elite of the city, the bride being the lovely young daughter of a Cuban planter, the groom a burly Negro. Nobody to the manor born has ever dreamed of objecting to this mingling of colors; therefore, when some newly arrived foreigner declares that nobody but those of his own complexion shall eat in a public dining-room, there is likely to be trouble.

THE WAR BEGAN.

When the war began the population of Cuba was a little more than one-third black; now the proportion is officially reckoned as 525,684 colored, against 1,631,600 white. In 1898 two Negroes were serving as secretaries in the Autonomist Cabinet. The last regiment that Blanco formed was of Negro volunteers, to whom he paid—or, rather, promised to pay, which is quite another matter, considering Blanco's habit—the unusual hire of $20 a month, showing his appreciation of the colored man as a soldier. If General Weyler evinced any partiality in Cuba, it was for the black Creole. During the ten years' war, his cavalry escort was composed entirely of colored men.

Throughout his latest reign in the Island he kept black soldiers constantly on guard at the gates of the government palace. While the illustrated papers of Spain were caricaturing the insurgents as coal-black demons with horns and forked toe nails, burning canefields and butchering innocent Spaniards, the Spanish General chose them for his bodyguards.

ONE OF THE GREATEST GENERALS.

One of the greatest Generals of the day, considering the environment, was Antonio Maceo, the Cuban mulatto hero, who, for two years, kept the Spanish army at bay or led them a lively quickstep through the western provinces to the very gates of Havana. As swift on the march as Sheridan or Stonewall Jackson, as wary and prudent as Grant himself, he had inspirations of military genius whenever a crisis arose. It is not generally known that Martinez Campos, who owed his final defeat at Calisea to Maceo, was a second cousin of this black man. Maceo's mother, whose family name was Grinan, came from the town of Mayari where all the people have Indian blood in their veins. Col. Martinez del Campos, father of General Martinez Campos, was once Military Governor of Mayari. While there he loved a beautiful girl of Indian and Negro blood, who belonged to the Grinan family, and was first cousin to Maceo's mother. Martinez Campos, Jr., the

Cuban Women Cavalry.

future General and child of the Indian girl, was born in Mayari. The Governor could not marry his sweetheart, having a wife and children in Spain, but when he returned to the mother country he took the boy along. According to Spanish law, the town in which one is baptized is recognized as his legal birthplace, so it was easy enough to legitimatize the infant Campos. He grew up in Spain, and when sent to Cuba as Captain-General, to his everlasting credit be it said, one of his first acts was to hunt up his mother. Having found her, old and poor, he bought a fine house in Campo Florida, the aristocratic suburb of Havana, established her there and cared for her tenderly till she died. The cousins, though on opposite sides of the war, befriended each other in many instances, and it is said that more than once Captain-General Campos owed his life to his unacknowledged relative.

HIS BROTHER CAPTURED.

The latter's half-brother, Jose Maceo, was captured early in the war and sent to the African prison Ceuta, whence he escaped later on with Quintin Bandera and others of his staff. The last named Negro Colonel is to-day a prominent figure. "Quintin Bandera" means "fifteen flags," and the appellation was bestowed upon him by his grateful countrymen after he had captured fifteen Spanish ensigns. Everybody seems to have forgotten his real name, and Quintin Bandera he will remain in history. While in the African penal settlement the daughter of a Spanish officer fell in love with him. She assisted in his escape and fled with him to Gibraltar. There he married his rescuer. She is of Spanish and Moorish descent, and is said to be a lady of education and refinement. She taught her husband to read and write and feels unbounded pride in his achievements.

The noted General Jesus Rabi, of the Cuban Army, is of the same mixed blood as the Maceos. Another well-known Negro commander was General Flor Crombet, whose patriotic deeds have been dimmed by his atrocious cruelties. Among all the officers swarming Havana none attracts more admiring attention than General Ducasse, a tall, fine-looking mulatto, who was educated at the fine military school of St. Cyr. He is of extremely polished manners and undeniable force of character, can make a brilliant address and has great influence among the masses. To eject such a man as he from a third-rate foreign restaurant in his own land would be ridiculous. His equally celebrated brother, Col. Juan Ducasse, was killed in the Pinar del Rio insurrection.

COLORED MEN'S ACHIEVEMENTS.

Besides these sons of Mars, Cuba has considered her history enriched by the achievements of colored men in peaceful walks of life. The

memory of Gabriel Concepcion de la Valdez, the
mulatto poet, is cherished as that of a saint.
He was accused by the Spanish government of
complicity in the slave insurrection of 1844, and
condemned to be shot in his native town, Matanzas.   One bright morning in May he stood by
the old statue of Ferdinand VII. in the Plaza
d'Armas, calmly facing a row of muskets, along
whose shining barrels the sun glinted.   The
first volley failed to touch a vital spot.   Bleeding from several wounds, he still stood erect,
and, pointing to his heart, said in a clear voice,
"Aim here!"   Another mulatto author, educator
and profound thinker was Antonio Medina, a
priest and professor of San Basilio the Greater.
He acquired wide reputation as a poet, novelist
and ecclesiastic, both in Spain and Cuba, and
was selected by the Spanish Academy to deliver
the oration on the anniversary of Cervantes'
death in Madrid.   His favorite Cuban pupil was
Juan Gaulberto Gomez, the mulatto journalist,
who has been imprisoned time and again for
offences against the Spanish press laws.   Senor
Gomez, whose home is in Matanzas, is now on
the shady side of 40, a spectacled and scholarly-
looking man.   After the peace of Zanjon he col-
laborated in the periodicals published by the
Marquis of Sterling.   In 1879 he founded in
Havana the newspaper "La Fraternidad," devoted to the interest of the colored race.   For
a certain fiery editorial he was deported to Ceuta

and kept there two years. Then he went to Madrid and assumed the management of "La Tribuna," and in 1890 returned to Havana and resumed the publication of "La Fraternidad."

ANOTHER EXILE.

Another beloved exile from the land of his birth is Senor Jose White. His mother was a colored woman of Matanzas. At the age of 16 years Jose wrote a mass for the Matanzas orchestra and gave his first concert. With the proceeds he entered the Conservatory of Paris, and in the following year won the first prize as violinist among thirty-nine contestants. He soon gained an enviable reputation among the most celebrated European violinists, and, covered with honors, returned to Havana in January of 1875. But his songs were sometimes of liberty, and in June of the same year the Spanish government drove him out of the country. Then he went to Brazil, and was President of the Conservatory of Music of Rio Janeiro.

One might go on multiplying similar incidents. Some of the most eminent doctors, lawyers and college professors in Cuba are more or less darkly "colored." In the humble walks of life one finds them everywhere, as carpenters, masons, shoemakers and plumbers. In the few manufacturies of Cuba a large proportion of the workmen are Negroes, especially in the cigar factories. In the tanneries of Pinar del Rio most of the workmen are colored, also in the saddle factories of Havana, Guanabacoa, Cardenas and other places.   Although the insurgent army is not yet disbanded, the sugar-planters get plenty of help from their ranks by offering fair wages.—"New York Sun."

FACTS ABOUT PORTO RICO TOLD IN SHORT PARAGRAPHS.

Porto Rico, the beautiful island which General Miles took under the American flag, has an area of 3,530 square miles.   It is 107 miles in length and 37 miles across.   It has a good telegraph line and a railroad only partially completed.

The population, which is not made up of so many Negroes and mulattoes as that of the neighboring islands, is about 900,000.   Almost all of the inhabitants are Roman Catholics.

It is a mountainous island, and contains forty-seven navigable streams.   The roads are merely paths beaten down by cattle.

Exports in 1887 were valued at $10,181,291; imports, $10,198,006.

Gold, copper, salt, coal and iron abound.

The poorer classes live almost entirely on a variety of highland rice, which is easily cultivated, as it requires no flooding.

One of the principal industries is grazing. St. Thomas is the market for fresh meat.

Corn, tobacco, sugar, coffee, cotton and potatoes constitute the principal crops.

There are no snakes, no beasts of prey, no noxious birds nor insects in the island.

The trees and grass are always green.

Rats are the great foe of the crops.

The natives often live to be one hundred years old.

The most beautiful flower on the island is the ortegon, which has purple blossoms a yard long.

Hurricanes are frequent on the north coast and very destructive.

Mosquitoes are the pest of the island.

Spanish is the language spoken, and education is but little esteemed.

Every man, no matter how poor, owns a horse and three or four gamecocks.

The small planter is called "Xivaro." He is the proud possessor of a sweetheart, a gamecock, a horse, a hammock, a guitar and a large supply of tobacco. He is quick-tempered but not revengeful.

Hospitality is the rule of the island. The peasants are astonished and hurt when offered money by travellers. San Juan Harbor is one of the best in the West Indies, and is said to be the third most strongly fortified town in the world, Halifax being the strongest and Cartagena, Spain, the second.

Ponce de Leon, between 1509 and 1518, killed off the natives.

The De Leon palace, built in 1511, is of great interest to tourists.

The climate is warm but pleasant. At night thick clothing is found comfortable.

All visiting and shopping are done after sundown.

Slavery was abolished in 1873.

The women are rather small and delicately formed. Many of them are considered very pretty.

Men and women ride horseback alike. Wicker baskets to carry clothes or provisions are hung on either side of the horse's shoulders. Back of these baskets the rider sits.

It is the custom of travellers on horseback to carry a basket-handled sword a yard and a quarter long, more as an ornament than as a means of defense.

The observance of birthdays is an island fashion that is followed by every one.

Upon the Rio Grande are prehistoric monuments that have attracted the attention of archaeologists.

In the towns houses are built with flat roofs, both to catch water and to afford the family a small roof garden.

All planters have town houses where they bring their families during the carnival season.

A large size photo of above picture can be had on application to P. H. Bauer, Photographer, Leavenworth, Kansas.

CHAPTER VII.

LIST OF COLORED REGIMENTS THAT DID ACTIVE SERVICE IN THE SPANISH-AMERICAN WAR, AND VOLUNTEER REGIMENTS.

Regulars.—Section 1104 of the Revised Statutes of the United States Congress provides that "the enlisted men of two regiments of Cavalry shall be colored men," and in compliance with this section the War Department maintains the organization of the Ninth and Tenth Cavalry, both composed of colored men with white officers.

Section 1108 of the Revised Statutes of Congress provides that "the enlisted men of two regiments of Infantry shall be colored men"; and in compliance with this section the War Department maintains the organization of the Twenty-fourth and Twenty-fifth Infantry, both composed of colored men with white officers.

The above regiments were the only colored troops that were engaged in active service in Cuba. There is no statute requiring colored artillery regiments to be organized, and there are, therefore, none in the regular army.

A LIST OF THE VOLUNTEER REGIMENTS.

Third North Carolina—All colored officers.

Sixth Virginia—White officers, finally, the colored officers resigned "under pressure," after which there was much trouble with the men, as they claimed to have enlisted with the understanding that they were to have colored officers.

Ninth Ohio—All colored officers; Col. Chas. Young, graduate of West Point.

Twenty-third Kansas—Colored officers.

Eighth Illinois—Under colored officers, and did police duty at San Luis, Cuba.

Seventh U. S. Volunteers.

Tenth U. S. Volunteers.

Eighth U. S. Volunteers.

Ninth U. S. Volunteers.

The conduct of the colored volunteers has been harshly criticized, and it is thought by some that the conduct of the volunteers has had some influence in derogation of the good record made by the regulars around Santiago. This view, however, we think unjust and ill-founded. There was considerable shooting of pistols and drunkenness among some regiments of volunteers, and it was not confined by any means to those of the colored race. The white volunteers were as drunk and noisy as the colored, and shot as many pistols.

The "Charlotte Observer" had the following

editorial concerning some white troops that passed through Charlotte, N. C.:

"Mustered-out West Virginia and New York volunteer soldiers, who passed through this city Saturday night, behaved on the train and here like barbarians, disgracing their uniforms, their States and themselves. They were drunk and disorderly, and their firing of pistols, destruction of property and theft of edibles was not as bad as their outrageous profanity and obscenity on the cars in the hearing of ladies. Clearly they are brutes when sober and whiskey only developed the vileness already in them."

By a careful comparison of the reports in the newspapers, we see a slight excess of rowdyism on the part of the whites, but much less fuss made about it. In traveling from place to place, if a white volunteer company fired a few shots in the air, robbed a fruit stand, or fussed with the bystanders at railroad stations, or drank whiskey at the car windows, the fact was simply mentioned in the morning papers, but if a Negro company fired a pistol a telegram was sent ahead to have mobs in readiness to "do up the niggers" at the next station, and at one place in Georgia the militia was called out by a telegram sent ahead, and discharged a volley into the car containing white officers and their families, so eager were they to "do up the nigger." At Nashville the city police are reported to have charged through the train clubbing the

Officers of the Ninth Ohio—Lieutenant Young in the Center.

colored volunteers who were returning home, and taking anything in the shape of a weapon away from them by force. In Texarcana or thereabouts it was reported that a train of colored troopers was blown up by dynamite. The Southern mobs seemed to pride themselves in assaulting the colored soldiers.

While the colored volunteers were not engaged in active warfare, yet they attained a high degree of discipline, and the CLEANEST AND MOST ORDERLY CAMP among any of the volunteers was reported by the chief sanitary officer of the government to be that of one of the colored volunteer regiments stationed in Virginia. It is to be regretted that the colored volunteers, especially those under Negro officers, did not have an opportunity to show their powers on the battlefield, and thus demonstrate their ability as soldiers, and so refreshing the memory of the nation as to what Negro soldiers once did at Fort Wagner and Milikin's Bend. The volunteer boys were ready and willing and only needed a chance to show what they could do.

POLICED BY NEGROES.

WHITE IMMUNES ORDERED OUT OF SANTIAGO, AND A COLORED REGIMENT PLACED IN CHARGE.

Washington, D. C., August 17, 1898.

Editor "Colored American":—The "Star" of this city published the following dispatch in its issue of the 16th inst. The "Washington Post" next morning published the same dispatch, omitting the last paragraph, and yet the "Post" claims to publish the news, whether pleasing or otherwise. The selection of the Eighth Illinois Colored Regiment for this important duty, to replace a disorderly white regiment, is a sufficient refutation of a recent editorial in the "Post," discrediting colored troops with colored officers. The Eighth Illinois is a colored regiment from Colonel down. The Generals at the front know the value of Negro troops, whether the quill-drivers in the rear do or not.

CHARLES R. DOUGLASS.

Following is the dispatch referred to by Major Douglass. The headlines of the "Star" are retained.

IMMUNES MADE TROUBLE—GENERAL SHAFTER ORDERS THE SECOND REGIMENT OUTSIDE THE CITY OF SANTIAGO—COLORED TROOPS FROM ILLINOIS ASSIGNED TO THE DUTY OF PRESERVING ORDER AND PROPERTY.

Santiago de Cuba, Aug. 16.—General Shafter to-day ordered the Second Volunteer Regiment of Immunes to leave the city and go into camp outside.

The regiment had been placed here as a garrison, to preserve order and protect property. There has been firing of arms inside of the town by members of this regiment, without orders, so far as known. Some of the men have indulged in liquor until they have verged upon acts of license and disorder. The inhabitants in some quarters have alleged loss of property by force and intimidation, and there has grown up a feeling of uneasiness, if not alarm, concerning them. General Shafter has, therefore, ordered this regiment into the hills, where discipline can be more severely maintained.

In place of the Second Volunteer Immune Regiment, General Shafter has ordered into the city the Eighth Illinois Volunteer Regiment of colored troops, in whose sobriety and discipline he has confidence, and of whose sturdy enforcement of order no doubt is felt by those in command.

SKETCH OF SIXTH VIRGINIA VOLUNTEERS.

The Sixth Virginia Volunteer Infantry, U. S. V., consisted of two battalions, first and second Battalion Infantry Virginia Volunteers (State militia), commanded respectively by Maj. J. B. Johnson and Maj. W. H. Johnson. In April, 1898, the war cloud was hanging over the land. Governor J. Hoge Tyler, of Virginia, under instructions from the War Department, sent to all Virginia volunteers, inquiring how many men in the respective commands were willing to enlist in the United States volunteer service in the war against Spain.

How many would go in or out of the United States?

Major John R. Lynch, Paymaster in U. S. Army.

COMMONWEALTH OF VIRGINIA.

Adjutant-General's Office,
Richmond, Va., April 19th, 1898.

General Order No. 8.

I.   Commanding officers of companies of Virginia Volunteers will, immediately upon the receipt by them of this order, assemble their respective companies and proceed to ascertain and report direct to this office, upon the form herewith sent and by letter, what officers and enlisted men of their companies will volunteer for service in and with the volunteer forces of the United States (not in the regular army) with the distinct understanding that such volunteer forces, or any portion thereof, may be ordered and required to perform service either in or out of the United States, and that such officer or enlisted man, so volunteering, agrees and binds himself to, without question, promptly obey all orders emanating from the proper officers, and to render such service as he may be required to perform, either within or beyond the limits of the United States.

II.   The Brigade Commander and the Regimental and Battalion Commanders will, without delay, obtain like information and make, direct to this office, similar reports, to those above required, with regard to their respective field, staff and non-commissioned staff officers and regimental or battalion bands, adopting the form herewith sent to the regiments.

III. By reason of the necessity in this matter, this order is sent direct, with copies to intermediate commanders.

By order of the Governor and Commander-in-Chief.

WM. NALLE,
Adjutant-General.

The companies of the First Battalion of Richmond and Second Battalion of Petersburg and Norfolk were the first to respond to the call and express a readiness to go anywhere in or out of the States with their own officers, and upon these conditions they were immediately accepted, and the following order was issued:

COMMONWEALTH OF VIRGINIA.

Adjutant-General's Office,
Richmond, Va., April 23, 1898.

General Orders No. 9.

The commanding officers of such companies as will volunteer for service in the volunteer army of the United States will at once proceed to recruit their respective companies to at least eighty-four enlisted men. Any company volunteering as a body, for such service, will be mustered in with its own officers.

By order of the Governor and Commander-in-Chief.   W. NALLE,
(Signed)   Adjutant-General.

Under date of June 1, 1898, S. O. 59, A. G. O., Richmond, Va., was issued directly to the commanding officers of the First and Second Battalion (colored), who had been specially designated by the President in his call, ordering them to take the necessary steps to recruit the companies of the respective battalions to eighty-four men per company, directing that care be taken to accept only men of good repute and able-bodied, and that as soon as recruited the fact should be reported by telegraph to the Adjutant-General of the State.

July 15th, 1898, Company "A," Attucks Guard, was the first company to arrive at Camp Corbin, Va., ten miles below Richmond. The company had three officers: Capt. W. A. Hawkins, First Lieutenant J. C. Smith, Lieutenant John Parham.

The other companies followed in rapid succession. Company "B" (Carney Guard), Capt. C. B. Nicholas; First Lieutenant L. J. Wyche, Second Lieutenant J. W. Gilpin. Company "C" (State Guard), Capt. B. A. Graves; First Lieutenant S. B. Randolph, Second Lieutenant W. H. Anderson. Company "D" (Langston Guard), Capt. E. W. Gould; First Lieutenant Chas. H. Robinson, Second Lieutenant Geo. W. Foreman. Company "E" (Petersburg Guard),

Major R. R. Wright, Paymaster in U. S. Army.

Capt. J. E. Hill; First Lieutenant J. H. Hill, Second Lieutenant Fred E. Manggrum. Company "F" (Petersburg), Capt. Pleasant Webb; First Lieutenant Jno. K. Rice, Second Lieutenant Richard Hill. Company "G," Capt. J. A. Stevens; First Lieutenant E. Thomas Walker, Second Lieutenant David Worrell. Company "H," Capt. Peter Shepperd, Jr.; First Lieutenant Jas. M. Collins, Second Lieutenant Geo. T. Wright. The regiment consisted of only eight companies, two battalions, commanded respectively by Major J. B. Johnson and Maj. W. H. Johnson, commanded by Lieutenant Colonel Richard C. Croxton, of the First United States Infantry. First Lieutenant Chas. R. Alexander was Surgeon. Second Lieutenant Allen J. Black, Assistant Surgeon.

Lieutenant W. H. Anderson, Company "C," was detailed as Adjutant, Ordinance Officer and Mustering Officer.

Lieutenant J. H. Gilpin, Company "B," was detailed as Quartermaster and Commissary of Subsistence.

On Monday, September 12, 1898, the command left Camp Corbin, Va., and embarked for Knoxville, Tenn., about 10 o'clock, the men traveling in day coaches and the officers in Pullman sleepers. The train was in two sections. Upon arrival at Knoxville the command was sent to Camp Poland, near the Fourteenth Michigan Regiment, who were soon mustered out. A few days after the arrival of the Sixth Virginia the Third North Carolina arrived, a full regiment with every officer a Negro. While here, in order to get to the city, our officers, wagons and men had to pass the camp of the First Georgia Regiment, and it was quite annoying to have to suffer from unnecessary delays in stores and other things to which the men were subject.

After the review by General Alger, Secretary of War, the Colonel of the Sixth Virginia received permission from headquarters of Third Brigade, Second Division, First Army Corps, General Rosser commanding, to move the camp to a point nearer the city, which was granted. Soon after the arrival of the Third North Carolina Regiment the First Georgia seemed disposed to attack the colored soldiers, so on a beautiful September evening some shots were fired into their camp by the First Georgia men and received quick response. After the little affair four Georgians were missing. The matter was investigated and the First Georgia was placed under arrest.

After the removal to a new portion of Camp Poland orders were received from the headquarters First Army Corps, Lexington, Ky., ordering a board of examiners for the following officers of the Sixth Virginia: Maj. W. H. Johnson; Second Battalion, Capt. C. B. Nicholas, Capt. J. E. Hill, Capt. J. A. C. Stevens, Capt.

E. W. Gould, Capt. Peter Shepperd, Jr., Lieutenants S. B. Randolph, Geo. T. Wright and David Worrell, for examination September 20, 1898. Each officer immediately tendered his resignation, which was at once accepted by the Secretary of War.

Under the rules governing the volunteer army, when vacancies occurred by death, removal, resignation or otherwise, the Colonel of a regiment had the power to recommend suitable officers or men to fill the vacancies by promotions, and the Governor would make the appointment with the approval of the Secretary of War. Many of the men had high hopes of gaining a commission; many of the most worthy young men of the State, who left their peaceful vocations for the rough service of war, for they were students, bookkeepers, real estate men, merchants, clerks and artists who responded to their country's call—all looking to a much desired promotion. But after many conflicting stories as to what would be done and much parleying on the part of the recommending power, the latter said there was none in the regiment qualified for the promotion. And thereupon the Governor appointed white officers to fill the vacancies created. A copy of the following was sent to the Governor of Virginia through "military channels," but never reached him; also to the Adjutant-General of the army through military channels:

Sixth Virginia Volunteer Infantry,
Second Battalion, Colored,
Camp Poland, Tenn.,
October 27th, 1898.

To the Adjutant-General, U. S. Army, Washington, D. C.

Sir:—We, the undersigned officers of the Sixth Virginia Volunteer Infantry, stationed at Camp Poland, Knoxville, Tenn., have the honor to respectfully submit to you the following:

Nine officers of this command who had served the State militia for a period ranging from five to twenty years were ordered examined. They resigned for reasons best known to themselves. We, the remaining officers, were sanguine that Negro officers would be appointed to fill these vacancies, and believe they can be had from the rank and file, as the men in the various companies enlisted with the distinct understanding that they would be commanded by Negro officers. We now understand through various sources that white officers have been, or are to be, appointed to fill these vacancies, to which we seriously and respectfully protest, because our men are dissatisfied. The men feel that the policy inaugurated as to this command should remain, and we fear if there is a change it will result disastrously to one of the best disciplined commands in the volunteer service. They are unwilling to be commanded by white officers and object to do what they did not agree to at first. That is, to be commanded by any other than officers of the same color. We furthermore believe that should the appointments be confirmed there will be a continual friction between the officers and men of the two races as has been foretold by our present commanding officer. We express the unanimous and sincere desire of seven hundred and ninety-one men in the command to be mustered out rather than submit to the change.

We therefore pray that the existing vacancies be filled from the rank and file of the command or by men of color. To all of which we most humbly pray.

(Signed)

J. B. JOHNSON, Major 6th Va. Vol. Inf.
PLEASANT WEBB, Capt. 6th Va. Vol. Inf.
BENJ. A. GRAVES, Capt. 6th Va. Vol. Inf.
JAS. C. SMITH, 1st Lt. 6th Va. Vol. Inf.
L. J. WYCHE, 1st Lt. 6th Va. Vol. Inf.
CHAS. H. ROBINSON, 1st Lt. 6th Va. Vol.
JOHN H. HILL, 1st Lt. 6th Va. Vol. Inf.
JNO. K. RICE, 1st Lt. 6th Va. Vol. Inf.
EDWIN T. WALKER, 1st Lt. 6th Va. Vol.
C. R. ALEXANDER, 1st Lt. and Surg. 6th Va. Vol. Inf.
JOHN PARHAM, 2nd Lt. 6th Va. Vol. Inf.
JAS. ST. GILPIN, 2nd Lt. 6th Va. Vol. Inf.
W. H. ANDERSON, 2nd Lt. 6th Va. Vol. Inf.
GEORGE W. FOREMAN, 2nd Lt. 6th Va. Vol. Inf.
FREDERICK E. MANGGRUM, 2nd Lt. 6th Va. Vol. Inf.
RICHARD HILL, 2nd Lt. 6th Va. Vol. Inf.
JAMES M. COLLIN, 2nd Lt. 6th Va. Vol. Inf.

Major J. B. Johnson,
of the Sixth Virginia Colored Volunteers.

FIRST ENDORSEMENT.

Headquarters 6th Va. Vol. Inf.
Second Battalion, Colored,

Camp Poland, Tenn., Oct. 28, 1898.

Respectfully forwarded.

I have explained to the officers who signed this paper that their application is absurd, but they seem unable to see the points involved.

The statement within that 791 men prefer to be mustered out rather than serve under white officers is based upon the alleged reports that each First Sergeant stated to his Captain that all the men of the company were of that opinion. The statement that the men "enlisted with the understanding that they would be commanded entirely by Negro officers," seems to be based upon the fact that when these companies were called upon by the State authorities they volunteered for service, etc., "with our present officers." These officers (nine of them) have since resigned and their places filled by the Governor of Virginia with white officers.

These latter have not yet reported for duty.

Further comment seems as unnecessary as the application itself is useless.

(Signed)   R. C. CROXTON,
                Lt.-Col. 6th Va. Vol. Inf. Com'd'g.

SECOND ENDORSEMENT.

Headquarters Third Brigade,
Second Division, First Army Corps,

Camp Poland, Tenn., Oct. 29, 1898.

Respectfully forwarded. Disapproved, as under the law creating the present volunteer forces the Governor of Virginia is the only authority who can appoint the officers of the 6th Va. Vol. Inf.

(Signed)   JAMES H. YOUNG,
Col. Third N. C. Vol. Inf. Com'd'g Brigade.

THIRD ENDORSEMENT.

Headquarters Second Division,
First Army Corps,

Camp Poland, Knoxville, Tenn., Oct. 31, 1898.

Respectfully returned to the Commanding General, Third Brigade.

The enclosed communication is in form and substance so contrary to all military practice and traditions that it is returned for file at Regimental Headquarters, 6th Va. Vol. Infantry.

By command of Colonel KUERT.

(Signed)   LOUIS V. CAZIARC,
Assistant Adjutant-General.

FOURTH ENDORSEMENT.

Headquarters Third Brigade,
Second Division, First Army Corps.

Respectfully transmitted to C. O., 6th Virginia, inviting attention to preceding Inst.

By order of Colonel YOUNG.

(Signed)   A. B. COLLIER,
Captain Assistant Adjutant-General.

A NEW LIEUTENANT FOR THE SIXTH VIRGINIA.

October 31st, 1898, the monthly muster was in progress. There appeared in the camp a new lieutenant—Lieut. Jno. W. Healey—formerly Sergeant-Major in the regular army. This was the first positive evidence that white officers would be assigned to this regiment. This was about 9 o'clock in the morning, and at Knoxville later in the day there were more arrivals. Then it was published that the following changes and appointments were made:

Company "D," First Battalion, was transferred to the Second Battalion; Company "F," of the Second Battalion, transferred to the First Battalion.

Major E. E. Cobell, commanding Second Battalion.

Captain R. L. E. Masurier, commanding Company "D."

Captain W. S. Faulkner, commanding Company "E."

Captain J. W. Bentley, commanding Company "G."

Captain S. T. Moore, commanding Company "H."

First Lieutenant Jno. W. Healey to Company "H."

First Lieutenant A. L. Moncure to Company "G."

Second Lieutenant Geo. W. Richardson, Company "G."

First Lieutenant Edwin T. Walker transferred to Company "C."

November 1st officers attempted to take charge of the men who offered no violence at all, but by their manner and conduct it appeared too unpleasant and unsafe for these officers to remain, so tendered their resignations, but they were withheld for a day.

The next day, November 2, 1898, it was thought best that the colored captains and lieutenants would drill the companies at the 9 o'clock drill. While on the field "recall" was sounded and the companies were brought to the headquarters and formed a street column. General Bates, commanding the Corps and his staff; Col. Kuert, commanding the Brigade and Brigade staff; Maj. Louis V. Caziarc, Assistant Adjutant-General; Lieut.-Col. Croxton and Maj. Johnson were all there and spoke to the men.

Colonel Kuert said: "Gentlemen, as commanding officer of the Brigade, I appear before you to-day asking you to do your duty; to be good soldiers, to remember your oath of enlistment, and to be careful as to the step you take, for it might cost you your life; that there are enough soldiers at my command to force you into submission should you resist. Now, if you intend to accept the situation and submit to these officers placed over you, at my command, you come to a right shoulder, and if you have any grievance, imaginary or otherwise, present through proper military channels, and if they are proper your wrongs will be adjusted."

"Right shoulder, Arms." Did not a man move. He then ordered them to be taken back to their company street and to "stack arms."

Before going to the company streets Major Caziarc spoke to the men as follows: "Forty years ago no Negro could bear arms or wear the blue. You cannot disgrace the blue, but you can make yourselves unworthy to wear it."

Then Maj. J. B. Johnson spoke to the men and urged upon them to keep in mind the oath of enlistment (which he read to them), in which they swore that they would "obey all officers placed over them"; that since the appointments had been made there was nothing for them to do but to accept the situation. At the conclusion of Maj. Johnson's talk to the men, Private Badger, Regimental tailor, stepped to the front

Third North Carolina Volunteers and Officers.

and gave the "rifle salute" and asked permission to say a word. It was granted. He said: "When we enlisted we understood that we would go with our colored officers anywhere in or out of this country, and when vacancies occurred we expected and looked for promotion, as was the policy of the Governor of Virginia toward other Virginia regiments." He was told that if the men had any grievance they could present it through military channels and it would be looked into. They never accepted Maj. Johnson's advice—returned to their company streets and were allowed to keep their guns. The Ordnance Officer was ordered to take all ammunition to the camp of the Thirty-first Michigan and place it in the guard-house.

The men had the freedom and pass privilege to and from the city.

November 19th the command was ordered to Macon, Ga., arriving at Camp Haskell next day, with 820 men and 27 officers.

Near the camp of the Sixth Virginia was that of the Tenth Immune Regiment, in which were many Virginia boys, some of whom had been members of some of the companies of the Sixth.

Some irresponsible persons cut down a tree upon which several men had been lynched. The blame naturally fell upon the Sixth Virginia. The regiment was placed under arrest and remained so for nineteen days. The first day the Third Engineers guarded the camp, but General

Wilson, the Corps commander, removed them and put colored soldiers to guard them. On the night of November 20th, at a late hour, the camp was surrounded by all the troops available while the men were asleep and the regiment was disarmed.

While all this was going on, the Thirty-first Michigan Regiment had been deployed into line behind a hill on the north, and the Fourth Tennessee had been drawn up in line on the east side of the camp ready to fire should any resistance be offered.

The men quietly submitted to this strange procedure, and did not know that Gatling guns had been conveniently placed at hand to mow them down had they shown any resistance. The Southern papers called them the mutinous Sixth, and said and did everything to place discredit upon them.

They were reviewed by General Breckinridge, General Alger, Secretary of War, and President McKinley, who applauded them for their fine and soldierly appearance.

COMMENTS ON THE THIRD NORTH CAROLINA REGIMENT.

Of all the volunteer regiments the Third North Carolina seemed to be picked out as the target for attack by the Georgia newspapers. The "Atlanta Journal," under large headlines,

"A Happy Riddance," has the following to say when the Third North Carolina left Macon. But the "Journal's" article was evidently written in a somewhat of a wish-it-was-so manner, and while reading this article we ask our readers to withhold judgment until they read Prof. C. F. Meserve on the Third North Carolina, who wrote after investigation.

The "Journal" made no investigation to see what the facts were, but dwells largely on rumors and imagination. It will be noted that President Meserve took the pains to investigate the subject before writing about it.

The "Atlanta Journal" says:

A HAPPY RIDDANCE.

"The army and the country are to be congratulated on the mustering out of the Third North Carolina Regiment.

"A tougher and more turbulent set of Negroes were probably never gotten together before. Wherever this regiment went it caused trouble.

"While stationed in Macon several of its members were killed, either by their own comrades in drunken brawls or by citizens in self-defense.

"Last night the mustered-out regiment passed through Atlanta on its way home, and during its brief stay here exhibited the same ruffianism and brutality that characterized it while in the service. But for the promptness and pluck of several Atlanta policemen these Negro ex-soldiers would have done serious mischief at the depot. Those who undertook to make trouble were very promptly clubbed into submission, and one fellow more obstreperous than the rest was lodged in the station house.

"With the exception of two or three regiments the Negro volunteers in the recent war were worse than useless. The Negro regulars, on the contrary, made a fine record, both for fighting and conduct in camp.

"The mustering out of the Negro volunteers should have begun sooner and have been completed long ago."

WHAT PRESIDENT CHARLES FRANCIS MESERVE SAYS.

President Charles Francis Meserve, of Shaw University, says:

"I spent a part of two days the latter part of December at Camp Haskell, near Macon, Ga., inspecting the Third North Carolina colored regiment and its camp and surroundings. The fact that this regiment has colored officers and the knowledge that the Colonel and quite a number of officers, as well as many of the rank and file, were graduates or former students of Shaw University, led me to make a visit to this regiment, unheralded and unannounced. I was just crossing the line into the camp when I was stopped by a guard, who wanted to know who I was and what I wanted. I told him I was a very small .piece of Shaw University, and that I wanted to see Colonel Young. After that sentence was uttered, and he had directed me to the headquarters of the Colonel, the regiment and the camp might have been called mine, for the freedom of everything was granted me.

"The camp is admirably located on a sandy hillside, near pine woods, and is dry and well drained. It is well laid out, with a broad avenue in the centre, intersected by a number of side streets. On one side of the avenue are the tents and quarters of the men and the canteen, and on the opposite side the officers' quarters, the hospital, the quartermasters' stores, the Y. M. C. A. tent, etc.

"Although the weather was unfavorable, the camp was in the best condition, and from the standpoint of sanitation was well-nigh perfect. I went everywhere and saw everything, even to the sinks and corral. Part of the time I was alone and part of the time an officer attended me. There was an abundant supply of water from the Macon water works distributed in pipes throughout the camp. The clothing was of good quality and well cared for. The food was excellent, abundant in quantity and well prepared. The beef was fresh and sweet, for it had not been 'embalmed.' The men were not obliged to get their fresh meat by picking maggots out of dried apples and dried peaches as has been the case sometimes in the past on our 'Wild West Frontier.' There were potatoes, Irish and sweet, navy beans, onions, meat, stacks of light bread,

Prof. Charles F. Meserve,
of Shaw University, Raleigh, N. C.,
Who investigated and made report on the Third N. C. Volunteers.

canned salmon, canned tomatoes, etc. These were not all served at one meal, but all these articles and others go to make up the army ration list.

"The spirit and discipline of officers and men was admirable, and reflected great credit upon the Old North State. There was an enthusiastic spirit and buoyancy that made their discipline and evolutions well-nigh perfect. The secret of it all was confidence in their leader. They believe in their colonel, and the colonel in turn believes in his men. Col. James H. Young possesses in a marked degree a quality of leadership as important as it is rare. He probably knows by name at least three-quarters of his regiment, and is on pleasant terms with his staff and the men in the ranks, and yet maintains a proper dignity, such as befits his official rank.

"On the last afternoon of my visit of inspection Colonel Young ordered the regiment drawn up in front of his headquarters, and invited me to address them. The Colonel and his staff were mounted, and I was given a position of honor on a dry-goods box near the head of the beautiful horse upon which the Colonel was mounted. Besides Colonel James H. Young, of Raleigh, were near me Lieutenant-Colonel Taylor, of Charlotte; Major Walker, of Wilmington; Major Hayward, of Raleigh; Chief Surgeon Dellinger, of Greensboro; Assistant Surgeons Pope, of Charlotte, and Alston, of Asheville; Capt. Durham, of Winston; Capt. Hamlin, of Raleigh; Capt. Hargraves, of Maxton; Capt. Mebane, of Elizabeth City; Capt. Carpenter, of Rutherfordton; Capt. Alexander, of Statesville; Capt. Smith, of Durham; Capt. Mason, of Kins-

ton, who served under Colonel Shaw at Fort
Wagner; Capt. Leatherwood, Asheville; Capt.
Stitt, of Charlotte; Capt. York, of Newbern, and
Quartermaster Lane, of Raleigh. That highly
respected citizen of Fayetteville, Adjutant
Smith, was in the hospital suffering from a
broken leg. I told them they were on trial, and
the success or failure of the experiment must
be determined by themselves alone; that godli-
ness, moral character, prompt and implicit obedience, as well as bravery and unflinching
courage, were necessary attributes of the true
soldier.

"The Y. M. C. A. tent is a great blessing to
the regiment, and is very popular, and aids in
every possible way the work of Chaplain Durham.

"The way Colonel Young manages the canteen cannot be too highly recommended. Or-
dinarily the term canteen is another name for
a drinking saloon, though a great variety of
articles, such as soldiers need, are on sale and
the profits go to the soldiers. But the canteen
of the Third North Carolina is a dry one. By
that I mean that spirituous or malt liquors are
not sold. Colonel Young puts into practice the
principles that have always characterized his
personal habits, and with the best results to
his regiment.

"I had the pleasure of meeting Capt. S. Bab-
cock, Assistant Adjutant-General of the Brigade,

who has known this regiment since it was mustered into the service. He speaks of it in the highest terms. I also met Major John A. Logan, the Provost Marshal, and had a long interview with him. He said the Third North Carolina was a well-behaved regiment and that he had not arrested a larger per cent. of men from this regiment than from any other regiment, and that I was at liberty to publicly use this statement.

"While in the sleeper on my way home I fell in with Capt. J. C. Gresham, of the Seventh Cavalry. Capt. Gresham is a native of Virginia, a graduate of Richmond College and West Point, and has served many years in the regular army. He was with Colonel Forsyth in the battle with the Sioux at Wounded Knee, South Dakota. I had met him previously, when I was in the United States Indian service in Kansas. He informed me that he mustered in the first four companies of the Third North Carolina, and the Colonel and his staff, and that he had never met a more capable man than Colonel Young.

"The Third North Carolina has never seen active service at the front, and, as the Hispano-American war is practically a closed chapter, it will probably be mustered out of the service without any knowledge of actual warfare. I thought, however, as I stood on the dry-goods box and gave them kindly advice, and looked down along the line, that if I was a soldier in a white regiment and was pitted against them, my regiment would have to do some mighty lively work to 'clean them out.'

"CHARLES FRANCIS MESERVE.
"Shaw University,
"Raleigh, N. C., Jan. 25, 1899."

THE TWENTY-FOURTH UNITED STATES INFANTRY.

By Sergeant E. D. GIBSON.

The Twenty-fourth United States Infantry was organized by act of Congress July 28, 1866. Reorganized by consolidation of the 38th and 41st regiments of infantry, by act of Congress, approved March 3, 1869. Organization of regiment completed in September, 1869, with headquarters at Fort McKavett, Texas.

Since taking station at Fort McKavett, headquarters of the regiment have been at the following places:

1870-71, Fort McKavett, Texas; 1872, Forts McKavett and Brown, Texas; 1873-74, Forts Brown and Duncan, Texas; 1875-76 Fort Brown, Texas; 1877-78, Fort Clark, Texas; 1879, Fort Duncan, Texas; 1880, Forts Duncan and Davis, Texas; 1881-87, Fort Supply, Ind. Ter.; 1888, Forts Supply and Sill, Ind. Ter., and Bayard, N. M.; 1889 to 1896, Forts Bayard, N. M., and

Douglas, Utah; 1897, Fort Douglas, Utah; 1898, Fort Douglas, Utah, till April 20, when ordered into the field, incident to the breaking out of the Spanish-American War. At Chickamauga Park, Ga., April 24 to 30; Tampa, Fla., May 2 to June 7; on board transport "S. S. City of Washington," en route with expedition (Fifth Army Corps) to Cuba, from June 9 to 25; at Siboney and Las Guasimas, Cuba, from June 25 to 30; occupied the immediate blockhouse hill at Fort San Juan, Cuba, July 1 to 10, from which position the regiment changed to a place on the San Juan ridge about one-fourth of a mile to the left of the blockhouse, where it remained until July 15, when it took station at yellow fever camp, Siboney, Cuba, remaining until August 26, 1898; returned to the United States August 26, arriving at Montauk Point, L. I., September 2, 1898, where it remained until September 26, when ordered to its original station, Fort Douglas, Utah, rejoining October 1, 1898.

FIELD AND STAFF OFFICERS.

Colonel.—Henry B. Freeman, under orders to join.

Lieutenant-Colonel. — Emerson H. Liscum, Brig.-Gen. Vols. On sick leave from wounds received in action at Fort San Juan, Cuba, July 1, 1898.

Majors.—J. Milton Thompson, commanding regiment and post at Fort Douglas, Utah.

Alfred C. Markley, with regiment, commanding post of Fort D. A. Russell, Wyoming.

Chaplain.—Allen Allenworth, Post Treasurer and in charge of schools.

Adjutant.—Joseph D. Leitch, recruiting officer at post.

Quartermaster.—Albert Laws.

On July 1, 1898, our regiment was not a part of the firing line, and was not ordered on that line until the fire got so hot that the white troops positively refused to go forward. When our commander, Lieutenant-Colonel E. H. Liscum, was ordered to go in he gave the command "forward, march," and we moved forward singing "Hold the Fort, for we are coming," and on the eastern bank of the San Juan River we walked over the Seventy-first New York Volunteer Infantry. After wading the river we marched through the ranks of the Thirteenth (regular) Infantry and formed about fifty yards in their front. We were then about six hundred yards from and in plain view of the blockhouse and Spanish trenches. As soon as the Spaniards saw this they concentrated all of their fire on us, and, while changing from column to line of battle (which took about eight minutes), we lost one hundred and two men, and that place on the river to-day is called "bloody bend." We had only one advantage of the enemy—that was our superior marksmanship. I was right of the battalion that led the charge and I directed my line against the center of the trench, which was on a precipice about two hundred feet high.

I was born December 4, 1852, in Wythe County, Virginia, and joined the army in Cincinnati, Ohio, November 22, 1869, and have been in the army continuously since. I served my first ten years in the Tenth Cavalry, where I experienced many hard fights with the Indians. I was assigned to the Twenty-fourth Infantry by request in 1880.

E. D. GIBSON,

Sergeant Co. G, 24th U. S. Infantry,

Presidio, California.

CHAPTER VIII.

SOME FACTS ABOUT THE PHILIPPINOS.

WHO AGUINALDO IS.

Emilio Aguinaldo was born March 22, 1869, at Cavite, Viejo.

When twenty-five years old he was elected Mayor of Cavite.

On August 21, 1896, Aguinaldo became leader of the insurgents. The revolution started on that day.

He fought four battles with the Spaniards and was victorious in all. He lost but ten men, to the Spaniards' 125.

On December 24, 1897, a peace was established between Aguinaldo and the Spanish.

Aguinaldo received $400,000, but the rest of the conditions of peace were never carried out.

In June Aguinaldo issued a proclamation, expressing a desire for the establishment of a native administration in the Philippines under an American protectorate.

In an interview with a "World" correspondent at that time he expressed himself as grateful to Americans.

In July, 1897, he issued a proclamation fixing the 12th day of that month for the declaration of the independence of the Philippines.

In November, 1897, Aguinaldo defied General Otis, refusing to release his Spanish prisoners.

The Cabinet on December 2, 1897, cabled General Otis to demand the release of the prisoners.

AGUINALDO THE MAN.

In his features, face and skull Aguinaldo looks more like a European than a Malay.

He is what would be called a handsome man, and might be compared with many young men in the province of Andalusia, Spain. If there be truth in phrenology, he is a man above the common. Friends and enemies agree that he is intelligent, ambitious, far-sighted, brave, self-controlled, honest, moral, vindictive, and at times cruel. He possesses the quality which friends call wisdom and enemies call craft. According to those who like him he is courteous, polished, thoughtful and dignified; according to those who dislike him he is insincere, pretentious, vain and arrogant. Both admit him to be genial, generous, self-sacrificing, popular and capable in the administration of affairs. If the opinion of his foes be accepted he is one of the greatest Malays on the page of history. If the opinion of his friends be taken as the criterion he is one of the great men of history irrespective of race.—"The Review of Reviews."

FACTS FROM FELIPE AGONCILLO'S LETTER IN "LESLIE'S MAGAZINE."

Sixty per cent. of the inhabitants of the Philippines can read and write.

Emilio Aguinaldo, Military Dictator of the Filipinos.

The women in education are on a plane with the men.

Each town of 5,000 inhabitants has two schools for children of both sexes. The towns of 10,000 inhabitants have three schools. There are technical training schools in Manila, Iloilo, and Bacoler. "In these schools are taught cabinet work, silversmithing, lock-smithing, lithography, carpentering, machinery, decorating, sculpture, political economy, commercial law, book-keeping, and commercial correspondence, French and English; and there is one superior college for painting, sculpture and engraving. There is also a college of commercial exports in Manila, and a nautical school, as well as a superior school of agriculture. Ten model farms and a meteorological observatory are conducted in other provinces, together with a service of geological studies, a botanical garden and a museum, a laboratory and military academy and a school of telegraphy."

Manila has a girl's school (La Asunción) of elementary and superior branches, directed by French, English and Spanish mothers, which teaches French, English literature, arithmetic, algebra, trigonometry, topography, physics, geology, universal history, geography, designing, music, dress-making and needle-work. The capital has besides a municipal school of primary instruction and the following colleges: Santa Ysabel, Santa Catolina, La Concordia,

Santa Rosa de la Looban, a hospital of San
Jose, and an Asylum of St. Vincent de Paul, all
of which are places of instruction for children.

Felipe Agoncillo,
Emissary of the Filipinos to the
United States.

Gen. Pio Pilar,
In charge of the insurgent forces which
attacked the American troops.

There are other elementary schools in the State
of Camannis, in Pasig, in Vigan and Jaro.

The entire conduct of the civilization of the
Philippines as well as local authorities are in
the hands of the Philipinos themselves. They

also had charge of the public offices of the government during the last century.

There is a medical school and a school for midwives.

"All the young people, and especially the boys, belonging to well-to-do families residing in the other islands go to Manila to study the arts and learn a profession. Among the natives, to be ignorant and uneducated is a shameful condition of degradation.

"The sons of the rich families began to go to Spain in 1854" to be educated.

When the Spaniards first went to the islands "they found the Philipinos enlightened and advanced in civilization." "They had foundries for casting iron and brass, for making guns and powder. They had their special writing with two alphabets, and used paper imported from China and Japan." This was in the early part of the sixteenth century. The Spanish government took the part of the natives against the imposition of exorbitant taxes and the tortures of the inquisition by the early settlers.

The highest civilization exists in the island of Luzon, but in some of the remote islands the people are not more than "enlightened." The population embraced in Aguinaldo's dominion is 10,000,000, scattered over a territory in area approaching 200,000 square miles. The Americans up to this time have conquered only about 143 square miles of this territory.

What takes place in the South concerning the treatment of Negroes is known in the Philippines. The Philipino government on the 27th of February, 1899, issued from Hong-Kong the following decree warning the Philipino people as follows:

"Manila has witnessed the most horrible outrages, the confiscation of the properties and savings of the people at the point of the bayonet, the shooting of the defenseless, accompanied by odious acts of abomination, repugnant barbarism and social hatred, worse than the doings in the Carolinas."

They are told of America's treatment of the black population, and are made to feel that it is better to die fighting than become subject to a nation where, as they are made to believe, the colored man is lynched and burned alive indiscriminately. The outrages in this country are giving America a bad name among the savage people of the world, and they seem to prefer savagery to American civilization, such as is meted out to her dark-skinned people.

CHAPTER IX.

RÉSUMÉ.

Should the question be asked, "How did the American Negroes act in the Spanish-American War?" the foregoing brief account of their conduct would furnish a satisfactory answer to any fair mind. In testimony of their valiant conduct we have the evidence, first, of competent eyewitnesses; second, of men of the white race; and third, not only white race, but men of the Southern white race, in America, whose antipathy to the Negro "with a gun" is well known, it being related of the great George Washington, who, withal, was a slave owner, but mild in his views as to the harshness of that system—that on his dying-bed he called out to his good wife: "Martha, Martha, let me charge you, dear, never to trust a 'nigger' with a gun." Again we have the testimony of men high in authority, competent to judge, and whose evidence ought to be received. Such men as General Joseph Wheeler, Colonel Roosevelt, General Miles, President McKinley. If on the testimony of such witnesses as these we have not "established our case," there must be something wrong with the jury. A good case has been established, however, for the colored soldier, out of the mouth of many witnesses. The colored troopers just did so well that praise could not be withheld from them even by those whose

education and training had bred in them prejudice against Negroes. It can no longer be
doubted that the Negro soldier will fight. In
fact, such has been their record in past wars
that no scruples should have been entertained
on this point, but the (late) war was a fresh
test, the result of which should be enough
to convince the most incredulous "Doubting
Thomases."

The greater portion of the American people
have confidence in the Negro soldier. This confidence is not misplaced—the American government can, in the South, organize an army of
Negro soldiers that will defy the combined
forces of any nation of Europe. The Negro
can fight in any climate, and does not succumb
to the hardships of camp life. He makes a
model soldier and is well-nigh invincible.

The Negro race has a right to be proud of
the achievements of the colored troopers in the
late Spanish-American war. They were the
representatives of the whole race in that conflict; had they failed it would have been a calamity charged up to the whole race. The race's
enemies would have used it with great effect.
They did not fail, but did their duty nobly—a
thousand hurrahs for the colored troopers of
the Spanish-American War!!

In considering their successful achievements,
however, it is well to remember that there were
some things the Negro had to forget while

facing Spanish bullets. The Negro soldier in bracing himself for that conflict must needs forget the cruelties that daily go on against his brethren under that same flag he faces death to defend; he must forget that when he returns to his own land he will be met not as a citizen, but as a serf in that part of it, at least, where the majority of his people live; he must forget that if he wishes to visit his aged parents who may perhaps live in some of the Southern States, he must go in a "Jim Crow" car; he must forget that the flag he fought to defend in Cuba does not protect him nor his family at home; he must forget the murder of Frazier B. Baker, who was shot down in cold blood, together with his infant babe in its mother's arms, and the mother and another child wounded, at Lake City, S. C., for no other offense than attempting to perform the duties of Postmaster at that place —a position given him by President McKinley; he must forget, also, the shooting of Loftin, the colored Postmaster at Hagansville, Ga., who was guilty of no crime, but being a Negro and holding, at that place, the post-office, a position given him by the government.

WHY THE AMERICAN GOVERNMENT DOES NOT PROTECT ITS COLORED CITIZENS.

It is due to the peculiar and complicated construction of the laws relating to STATES

Convent at Cavite, Where Aguinaldo Was Proclaimed President of the Philippine Republic (June, 1898).

RIGHTS. The power to punish for crimes against citizens of the different States is given by construction of the Constitution of the United States to the courts of the several States. The Federal authorities have no jurisdiction unless the State has passed some law abridging the rights of citizens, or the State government through its authorized agents is unable to protect its citizens, and has called on the national government for aid to that end, or some United States official is molested in the discharge of his duty. Under this subtle construction of the Constitution a citizen who lives in a State whose public opinion is hostile becomes a victim of whatever prejudice prevails, and, although the laws may, in the letter, afford ample protection, yet those who are to execute them rarely do so in the face of a hostile public sentiment; and thus the Negroes who live in hostile communities become the victims of public sentiment. Juries may be drawn, and trials may be had, but the juries are usually white, and are also influenced in their verdicts by that sentiment which declares that "this is a white man's government," and a mistrial follows. In many instances the juries are willing to do justice, but they can feel the pressure from the outside, and in some instances the jurors chosen to try the cases were members of the mob, as in the case of the coroner's jury at Lake City.

It is the duty of a State Governor, when he finds public sentiment dominating the courts and obstructing justice, to interfere, and in case he cannot succeed with the sheriff and posse comitatus, then to invoke National aid. But this step has never yet been taken by any Governor of the States in the interest of Negro citizenship. Some of the State Governors have made some demonstration by way of threats of enforcing the law against those who organize mobs and take the law into their own hands; and some of the mob murderers have been brought to trial, which, in most cases, has resulted in an acquittal for the reason that juries have, as aforestated, chosen to obey public sentiment, which is not in favor of punishing white men for lynching Negroes, rather than obey the law; and cases against the election laws and for molesting United States officials have to be tried in the district where these offences occur, and, the juries being in sympathy with the criminals, usually acquit, or there is a mistrial because they cannot all agree.

That Mobocracy is Supreme in many parts of the Union is no longer a mooted question. It is a fact, and one that forebodes serious consequences, not only to the Negro, but to any class of citizens who may happen to come into disfavor with some other class. The sad feature of this is that the condition appears to be getting worse.

What the Negro should do under such circumstances must be left to the discretion of the individuals concerned. Some advise emigration, but that is impracticable, en masse, unless some suitable place could be found where any considerable number might go, and not fare worse. The colored people will eventually leave those places where they are maltreated, but "whether it is better to suffer the ills we now bear than flee to those we know not of," is the question. The prevailing sentiment among the masses seems to be to remain for the present where they are, and through wise action, and appeals to the Court of Enlightened Christian Sentiment, try to disarm the mob. There is no doubt a class of white citizens who regret such occurrences, and from their natural horror of bloodshed, and looking to the welfare and reputation of the communities in which such outrages occur, and feeling that withal the Negro makes a good domestic and farm hand, will, and do counsel against mob violence. In many places where mobs have occurred such white citizens have been invaluable aids in saving the lives of Negroes from mob violence; and trusting that these friends will increase and keep up their good work, the Negro has seldom ever left the scene of mob violence in any considerable numbers, the home ties being strong, and he instinctively loves the scene of his birth. He loves the white men who were boys with him, whose faces he

has smiled on from infancy, and he would rather
not sever those friendly ties. A touching incident is related in reference to a colored man in
a certain town where a mob was murdering
Negroes right and left, who came to the door
of his place of business, and seeing the face of
a young white man whom he had known from
his youth, asked protection for his wife and
five children. The reply came with an oath,
"Get back into that house or I will put a bullet
into you." The day before this these two men
had been "good friends," had "exchanged
cigars"—but the orders of the mob were
stronger in this instance than the ties of long
years of close friendship. Another instance,
though, will show how the mob could not control the ties of friendship of the white for the
black. It was the case of a colored man who
was blacklisted by a mob in a certain city, and
fled to the home of a neighboring white friend,
who kept him in his own house for several days
until escape was possible, and in the meantime
summoned his white neighbors to guard the
black man's family—threatening to shoot down
the first member of the mob who should enter the
gate, because, as he said, "you have no right
to frighten that woman and her children to
death." Such acts as this assure the Negroes in
places where feeling runs against them that perhaps they may be fortunate enough to escape
the violence of the terrible race hatred that is

now running riot in this country. In this connection it is well to remark that kindness will win in the long run with the Negro race, and make them the white man's friend. Those States where Negroes are being burned are sowing to the wind and will ere long reap the whirlwind in the matter of race hatred. Criminal assaults were not characteristic of the Negro in the days of slavery, because as a rule there was friendship between master and slave—the slave was too fond of his master's family but to do otherwise than protect it; but the situation is changed—instead of kindness the Negro sees nothing but rebuff on every hand; he feels himself a hated and despised race without country or protection anywhere, and the brute-spirit rises in those who, by their make-up and training, cannot keep it down—then follows murder, outrage, rape. It is true that only a few do these things, but those few are the natural products of the American system of oppression, and the wonder is, when the question is viewed philosophically, that there are so few. The conclusion here reached is that these States will not get rid of their brutes by burning them and taking the charred embers home as relics, but rather by treating the Negro population with more kindness and showing them that there is some hope for Negro citizenship. The Negroes know that white men have been known to rape colored girls, but that never has there been a

Church of San Sebastiano, Manilla.

suggestion of lynching or burning for that. And they feel despondent, for they know the courts are useless in such cases, and this jug-handle enforcement of lynch law is breeding its own bad fruits on the Negro race as well as making more brutal the whites. It is estimated that the whites have killed 10,000 Negroes in various ways since the Civil War, and that there has been only one white man hung for murder of a Negro, while, on the other hand, scarcely a Negro can escape who kills a white man, even if done in self-defense. My advice, then, to our white friends is to try "kindness" as a remedy for race troubles, and I am convinced of the force of this remedy from what I know of the occurrence of assaults and murders in those States where the Negroes are made to feel that they are citizens and are at home.

SUFFRAGE IN NORTH CAROLINA.

("Washington Post," Feb. 20, 1899.)

The amendment to the Constitution of North Carolina, which has for its object the limitation of the suffrage in the State, appears to have been modeled on the new Louisiana laws and operates a gross oppression and injustice. It is easy to see that the amendment is not intended to disfranchise the ignorant, but to stop short with the Negro; to deny to the illiterate black man the right of access to the ballot box and yet to leave the way wide open to the equally illiterate whites. In our opinion the policy thus indicated is both dangerous and unjust. We expressed the same opinion in connection with the Louisiana laws, and we see no reason to amend our views in the case of North Carolina. The proposed arrangement is wicked. It will not bear the test of intelligent and impartial examination. We believe in this case, as in that of Louisiana, that the Federal Constitution has been violated, and we hope that the people of North Carolina will repudiate the blunder at the polls.

We realize with sorrow and apprehension that there are elements at the South enlisted in the work of disfranchising the Negro for purposes of mere party profit. It has been so in Louisiana, where laws were enacted under which penniless and illiterate Negroes cannot vote, while the ignorant and vicious classes of whites are enabled to retain and exercise the franchise. So far as we are concerned—and we believe that the best element of the South in every State will sustain our proposition—we hold that, as between the ignorant of the two races, the Negroes are preferable. They are conservative; they are good citizens; they take no stock in social schisms and vagaries; they do not consort with anarchists; they cannot be made the tools and agents of incendiaries; they constitute the solid, worthy, estimable yeomanry of the South. Their influence in government would be infinitely more wholesome than the influence of the white sansculotte, the riff-raff, the idlers, the rowdies, and the outlaws. As between the Negro, no matter how illiterate he may be, and the "poor white," the property-holders of the South prefer the former. Excepting a few impudent, half-educated, and pestiferous pretenders, the Negro masses of the South are honest, well-meaning, industrious, and safe citizens. They are in sympathy with the superior race; they find protection and encouragement with the old slave-holding class; if left alone, they would furnish the bone and sinew of a secure and progressive civilization. To disfranchise this class and leave the degraded whites in possession of the ballot would, as we see the matter, be a blunder, if not a crime.

The question has yet to be submitted to a popular vote. We hope it will be decided in the negative. Both the Louisiana Senators are on record as proclaiming the unconstitutionality of the law. Both are eminent lawyers, and both devoted absolutely to the welfare of the South. We can only hope, for the sake of a people whom we admire and love, that this iniquitous legislation may be overruled in North Carolina as in Louisiana.

WHAT COURAGE! WHAT AN EXAMPLE OF FAITHFULNESS TO DUTY

did the colored troopers exhibit in forgetting

all these shortcomings to themselves and race of their own government when they made those daring charges on San Juan and El Caney!! They were possessed with large hearts and sublime courage. How they fought under such circumstances, none but a divine tongue can answer. It was a miracle, and was performed, no doubt, that good might come to the race in the shape of the testimonials given them as appears heretofore in this book. Their deeds must live in history as an honor to the Negro race. Let them be taught to the children. Let it be said that the Negro soldier did his duty under the flag, whether that flag protects him or not. The white soldier fought under no such sad reflections—he did not, after a hard-fought battle, lie in the trenches at night and dream of his aged mother and father being run out of their little home into the wintry blasts by a mob who sought to "string them up" for circulating literature relating to the party of William Mc-Kinley—the President of the United States— this was the colored soldier's dream, but he swore to protect the flag and he did it. The colored soldier has been faithful to his trust; let others be the same. If Negroes who have other trusts to perform do their duty as well as the colored soldiers, there will be many revisions in the scale of public sentiment regarding the Negro race in America—many arguments will be overthrown and the heyday towards Negro-citizenship will begin to dawn—there are other battles than those of the militia.

THE SOLUTION OF THE PROBLEM IS IN THE RACE'S OWN HANDS.

They must climb up themselves with such assistance as they can get. The race has done well in forty-six years of freedom, but it could have done better; banking on the progress already made, the next thirty years will, no doubt, show greater improvement than the past —time, time, time, which some people seem to take so little into account, will be the great adjuster of all such problems in the future as it has been in the past. Many children of the white fathers of the present day will read the writing of their parents and wonder at their shortsightedness in attempting to fix the metes and bounds of the American Negro's status. We feel reluctant to prophesy, but this much we do say, that fifty years from now will show a great change in the Negro's condition in America, and many of those who now predict his calamity will be classed wtih the fools who said before the Negro was emancipated that they would all perish within ten years for lack of ability to feed and clothe themselves. The complaint now with many of those who oppose the Negro is not because he lacks ability, but rather because he uses too much and sometimes gets the situation that they want. This is preeminently so from a political standpoint. So as to the prob-

Filipino Lady of Manila.

lem of the Negro's imbibing the traits of civilization, that point is settled by what he has already
done, and the untold obstacles which are being
constantly put in his way by those who fear his
competition. The question then turns not so
much on what shall be done with the Negro as
upon "what shall be done with the white men"
who are so filled with prejudice that neither
law nor religion restrains their bloody hands
when the Negro refuses to get into what is
called "his place," which place is that of a
menial; and often there seems no effort even
to put the Negro in any particular "place" save
the grave, as many of the lynchings and murders appear to be done either for the fun of
shooting some one, or else with extermination
in view. There is no attempt at a show of
reason or right. The mob spirit is growing—
prejudice is more intense. Formerly it was confined to the rabble, now it has taken hold of
those of education and standing. Red shirts
have entered the pulpits, and it is a matter
boasted of rather than condemned—the South
is not the only scene of such outrages. Prejudice is not confined to one section, but is, no
doubt, more intense in the Southern States, and
more far-reaching in its effects, because it is
there that the Negroes, by reason of the large
numbers in proportion to the other inhabitants,
come into political competition with the whites
who revolt at the idea of Negro officers, whether

they are elected by a majority of citizens or not. The whites seem bent on revolution to prevent the force and effect of Negro majorities. Whether public sentiment will continue to endorse these local revolutions is the question that can be answered only by time. Just so long as the Negro's citizenship is written in the Constitution and he believes himself entitled to it, just so long will he seek to exercise it. The white man's revolution will be needed every now and then to beat back with the Winchester the Negro's aspirations. The Negro race loves progress, it is fond of seeing itself elevated, it loves office for the honor it brings and the emoluments thereof, just as other progressive races do. It is not effete, looking back to Confucius; it is looking forward; it does not think its best days have been in the past, but that they are yet to come in the future; it is a hopeful race, teachable race; a race that absorbs readily the arts and accomplishments of civilization; a race that has made progress in spite of mountains of obstacles; a race whose temperament defied the worst evils of slavery, both African and American; a race of great vitality, a race of the future, a race of destiny.

In closing this résumé of this little work it is proper that I should warn the younger members of the race against despondency, and against the looseness of character and habits that is singularly consequential of a despondent spirit. Do not be discouraged, give up and throw away brilliant intellects, because of seeming obstacles, but rather resolve to "be something and do something in spite of obstacles."

"It was not by tossing feather balls into the air that the great Hercules gained his strength, but by hurling huge bowlders from mountain tops 'that his name became the synonym of manly strength.' So the harder the struggle the greater the discipline and fitness. If we cannot reach success in one way, let us try another. 'If the mountain will not come to Mahomet, let Mahomet go to the mountain.'"

Self-made men are usually strong characters —the race needs strong characters, it needs reliable men who will help live down the reputation that has already been made for us by the lick-spittle, and jig dancers. When high character marks the majority of the race, sentiment will change in our favor, and we will no longer be measured by the vices of the vicious, but by the virtues of the majority. Nothing tells for progress like self-respect. Money without it will not solve the problem, let there be both.

The South is a Good Place for the Negro to Live, provided, however, the better class of citizens will rise up and demand that lynchings and mobs shall cease, and that the officers of the law shall do their duty without prejudice. The only way to suppress mob violence is to make punishment for the leaders in it sure and certain. The reason we have mobs is because the leaders of them know they will not be punished. The enforcement of the law against lynchers will break it up.

The white ministers should take up the cause of justice rather than endorse the red shirts, or carry a Winchester themselves. They should be the counselors of peace and not the advocates of bloodshed. Most of them, no doubt, do regret the terrible deeds committed by mobs on helpless and innocent people, but it is a question as to whether or not they would be suffered by public sentiment to "cry aloud" against them. It takes moral courage to face any evil, but it must be faced or dire consequences will follow of its own breeding. Our last word then is an appeal to our BROTHERS IN WHITE, in the pulpit, that they should rally the people together for justice and condemn mob violence. The Negroes do not ask social equality, but civil equality; let the false notions that confound civil rights with social rights be dispelled, and advocate the civil equality of all men, and the problem will be solved.

Edmund Burke says that "war never leaves where it found a nation"; applying this to the American nation with respect to the Negro it is to be hoped that the late war will leave a better feeling toward him, especially in view of the glorious record of the Negro soldiers who participated in that conflict.

INDEX—PART I.

INDEX—PART II.

400